Discover the key to never-failing strength
in the time you spend alone.
Small prayer
You life will be transformed.

January 2013

Ryu, Kwang Su

When are you the happiest?

Like the few photos

that capture a long story

or a fleeting memory.

No matter how many pictures I take, no matter how much time passes, and how much experience I gain, I do not seem to get any better getting my picture taken. Each time, the photographer always says, "Pastor, please smile!!! Cheeeeeeese!" And each time, I end up with the corners of my lips curled up in an awkward grin or my eyes sheepishly shut. It was no different when I was young. Even though a long time has passed, smiling brightly is still awkward for me. However, just because my expression is stern does not mean that I am indifferent or gruff on the inside. It would not be an exaggeration to say that my expression is a sort of "poker face." This is because, more than anyone else, I have had to deal with ridiculous situations, exasperating incidents, misunderstanding that would have made the "old me" want to smash something, and events that leave me standing with my mouth wide open. Having to deal with all kinds of daily ups and downs leaves me exhausted. Perhaps, that is why I developed the habit of maintaining a single composure that has now become my fixed expression.

These days there are many people inside and outside of church talking about "healing" and many turn their ears to it as well. This reflects how many people there are struggling through their lives with heavy hearts, racked by scars and trauma. People lost in depression not able to sense the joy of living, people who appear to be successful yet are flailing about in the quicksand of addiction and corruption, people suffering from all kinds of unknown diseases; there are people who need healing everywhere. In one sense, it is a good thing when you can actually see the suffering and pain with your eyes; the hidden diseases of the heart and soul are the bigger problem. Most people may look like they are doing well but in actually, you never know if they are simply well adjusted or only appear to have adjusted well. People can always package themselves and act differently from their true inner self. When there is a clear disparity between their present reality and their ideal or when their true self becomes too dissociated from the face they show others, the diseases of the heart come calling. Furthermore, the diseases of the heart remain hidden in the unconscious, only to explode to the surface at any given moment.

Is there a way to solve this? Simply put, it can be solved through the Gospel. However, realistically applying the Gospel to your life is not that simple. The reason is that the countless things you have heard, seen, and believed that were not the Gospel have been imprinted inside your conscious and unconscious. Then your thinking must change first. Our thoughts are tainted by the views of people who think money is everything and we meet many people who recklessly live their lives without any balance or plans. The way to enjoy the Gospel inside your life is the "filling of the Holy Spirit." Perhaps this might seem like an abstract phrase but that would only be true if you do not know its true meaning.

Time passes so quickly. With the resolution and passion for preaching the Gospel, I raced all over the nation – Busan, Seoul, Daegu, Gwangju, Daejeon. I traveled throughout Los Angeles, Washington D.C., New York, St. Petersburg, Bishkek, Paris, Madrid, Frankfurt, Toronto, Valencia, Osaka, Tokyo, Hong Kong, Manila, Sydney, Kaohsiung - meeting countless evangelists who love the Gospel and logging in well over a million miles. Reflecting back on my college years when I tearfully closed the door to my dreams of studying in America, I was able to confirm once again how much my life has changed since then. Unable to go when I wanted to back then and now being sent by God to the places that God desires, what has brought about this great difference?

It is not bad to make up your mind to pray and actually do it. However, what would happen if whatever you did was prayer itself? For example, there is a cruise ship called Costa Fascinosa. This cruise line operates out of 260 ports all over the world in the Mediterranean Sea, North Europe, the Black Sea, the Canary Islands, South America, and the Caribbean. When you board this cruise ship, you go in and out of ports following the cruise route and ultimately, reach your destination no matter what you do or how you spend your time on board. You can eat your meals depending on your preferences or tastes, you can read a newspaper, you can rest on the comfy coach in your stateroom, or even swim in the pool. You can sleep for days or even take a tour of the town when you the ship calls to port; everything is all right. Everything I do, everywhere I go, every person I meet, and everything that happens around me is aligned in the same direction. I believe this is true prayer. No matter what you do, if you reach that level of prayer, there is no reason to become so attached to whether answers spread out before you or take their time in coming.

With the heart of capturing life's important moments and developing them to place inside an album so that all can easily see, I have organized the innumerous thoughts about prayer, perhaps the most important thing we have in our lives. This is not a book filled with many tidbits to take away with you. As you read this book, shed the layers of misunderstanding you have regarding prayer, one by one, and lighten your heart. With each page you turn, cast off one by one, the heavy sense of obligation that makes you say, "I know I should pray" and dispel the misgivings that make you think, "Nothing happens even if I do pray." And may you close the final chapter of this book feeling unburdened and free.

The reason the prayer we pray
when we are alone is important
is because that is when
our child-like prayers flow
from our hearts.

Chapter 01

The reason
people say
prayer is hard

New answers in your quiet time

Sensing a lack of communication, families are clamoring for more quality time together. Teenagers in their "rebellious stage" are busy texting with their friends, lost in games, or cooped up in their rooms preoccupied with who knows what, showing no signs of ever coming out. Affection and interest between spouses have dwindled to the point where a kiss or a hug seem like childish actions displayed in the distant memories from their newlywed years. This is how each day passes and now it has become the familiar and commonplace way of life.

My very own quiet time....

There are people who spend too much time alone, feeling uncomfortable around others. They pass their time in solitude feeling depressed and left out. Conversely, there are people who cannot stand being alone. Surrounding by many people, chatting away the hours gives them a sense of pleasure. Teenagers obsessed with spending all their time with their friends cannot do well in school and it seems as if they have no clue how to think for themselves. The psychologist Mihaly Csikszentmihali reveals in his book <Finding Flow> that the average person spends one third of his waking hour alone. He posits that spending too much time alone is bad but so is too little time alone.

However, the important fact is that everyone has "time spent alone," and the quality of your life will differ vastly depending on how you spend that time. In living our lives, one on one time spent with God is absolutely necessary. The reason I used "your own quiet time" is because I wanted to emphasize that all of us must receive our own personal answers. Make your own important time. You may have "flesh and blood" family members or friends who are closer than a brother; however, they cannot take responsibility for your spiritual health. You must receive grace from God.

Experiencing God's grace in your time of need through worship, conversing intimately with God in your life, turning your ear to God's voice are all blessings the child of God should rightfully enjoy.

If you can meet God because of a hardship?

Although he was hated and ostracized by his brothers, although he was sold as a slave to a strange land, and even though he was framed and went to prison, Joseph had the mystery of being with God in prayer. Through his "quiet time," he was able to interpret the great stormy trials and awful hardships with the eyes of faith and accept them as meaningful experiences. The folly of his hot-blooded youth trapped Moses in failure, but when he looked to God and saw God's historic desire, works arose. When he met God face to face and saw God's intention, God entrusted the Israelites into Moses' hands. When David was on the run, hiding out without a moment of peace or rest, he never forgot to make time to quietly converse with God. He was able to express and confess in psalms the overwhelming grace and love he received from God.

• Psalm 39:7
And now, O Lord, for what do I wait? My hope is in you.

• Psalm 62:1
For God alone my soul waits in silence; from him comes my salvation.

• Psalm 131:2
But I have calmed and quieted my soul,

like a weaned child with its mother;
like a weaned child is my soul within me.

How much personal and important time you spend with God will determine your future. This might sound cold but speaking frankly, there is no one who can help you. Being human, it is not easy to overstep the limitations you face time and again, and going to the extent of denying yourself for someone else's sake is something that is far easier said than done.

Therefore, how much time you spend within God's covenant is very important. When you meditate, not only your spiritual and mental health but even the rhythm of your physical body can be restored. The Word of God is living and active, sharper than any two edged sword, piercing to the division of soul and of spirit, of joints and of marrow, and discerning the thoughts and intentions of the heart. Gaining strength through the time you spend meditating deeply on the Word and seeking God's will is rightful. "But those who hope in The Lord will renew their strength."Isaiah 40:31 God has promised this to us.

Make your own quiet time and sincerely pray before God. Make that your happiest experience on earth. Do it joyfully without anyone having to tell you to do it and wisely guard it

If you can pray
for what God desire,

you will be the most free
and secure person in the world.

You set your wants, your desires
as your prayer topics
and badger God to answer this way or that way.

Just like a toddler taking her first steps,
pulls on her mother's hand
and pesters her to go to the uneven and rocky path.

The mother waits
until her child has the strength walk
and run on her own.

against anyone who would slyly steal that time away from you. If you have not experienced this mystery yet, then what a blessing it is that you have picked up this book.

Is there a certain type of prayer that gets answered?

When we pray in front of people, we are definitely mindful of our surroundings. Even though our faith is strong and we have been a believer for a long time, just the act of standing in front of other people finds us using more elaborate words and easily becoming distracted. The reason the prayer we pray when we are alone is important is because that is when our child-like prayers flow from our hearts. When no one is watching is when I am the truest form of the real me.

Even people who do not know God pray

I was on a plane to an overseas conference when a lovely and refined elderly lady sat next to me. She had a serene face and there was a ring on her finger. All throughout the flight, she twisted her ring and chanted a prayer. Her ability to concentrate for so long was quite amazing and I was also surprised because her actions did not make her appear fanatical but rather graceful.

You can often see older women who have Buddhist prayer beads wrapped around their arms when you ride the subway or the bus. Devout Buddhists offer their requests as they bow a thousand, even three thousand times. However, all that zeal does appear to produce results.

I have not met many Christians who have concrete prayer. People who have the ability to make good luck charms can divine your life and fortune by looking at your palms or facial features. However, the people who claim to believe in God somehow look anxious and seem wearied by the cares of life. They are so busy that they cannot spare a moment to pray or more often, they sit around staring blankly not knowing how to pray.

There is a type of prayer that is answered

There was a time when going to the mountain to pray was the trend. There is nothing wrong with going up to a prayer retreat center situated halfway up the side of the mountain, breathing in the clean air and praying, but only being able to pray when you go to the mountain or feeling like the prayer said on the mountain side are real prayers with a greater chance of being answered is a grave misconception. Students, employees, presidents of companies, mothers with children, housewives, heads of families cannot spend their days going in and out of prayer retreat centers.

A remote location and time set apart to pray can seem to be ideal conditions. However, the more important and necessary prayer is the prayer you pray when you are alone and what is even more key is the content of your prayers. There are people who designate their hopes and desires as prayer topics and plead with, even demand God to answer this way or that way. On top of that, they even go on a food strike starving themselves until God decides to grant them an answer out of fear that they might actually hurt themselves. However, are you aware that there is a separate prayer topic that God is happy to answer?

As a child of God, there are countless blessing inside the Gospel for you to enjoy. You are entitled to enjoy them. This is prayer. Praying as you ruminate on your blessings as a child of God is the prayer that is answered. There is no more intimate expression of God's love than that He is with us, unconditionally and unchangingly. Even amidst your ever changing circumstances, even when the sense of shame that comes from your inferiority complex and anxiety over why "things never work out for me" come sweeping over your soul, God is with you.

And of course, God is still with you when you are praised and complimented to the point of embarrassment and even when true peace and happiness make your heart feel like it will burst. This is the blessing of Immanuel.

Prayer is to be keenly aware that God is with you. The more you pray, the Holy Spirit leads you and you can concretely sense His working. There is no greater or more solid guarantee than the Almighty God becoming your master. This must be the underlying blessing in order to receive God's unique answers no matter what happens.

Of course, there is a type of prayer that gets answers, but there are times when answers come from places you never expected. Answers come through your daily life and through meetings. Have you ever experienced a blessed meeting that you would not exchange for any amount of money? Perhaps this may not be best expression, but there are a lot of "strange" people around us. There are people who bring spiritual confusion through insults and sophism, people who add burdens to your heart or always leave you with a deeper scar every time you meet them, people who lead you astray from the upright lifestyle, and people who plant false knowledge and trust.

If you do not have your time of prayer today and do not

receive the guidance of the Holy Spirit, you will be prone to making mistakes in your meetings and their influence and repercussions in your life can be far-reaching. Conversely, God can work upon His children who realized the mystery of the Gospel, through the same unexpected meetings.

For example, if you were the CEO of a company, who would you be more interested in, the person who is blinded by his own motives and avarice or the person who understands and follows the company's thoughts and principles? Rather than the person whose interests lie elsewhere, you would clearly give more opportunities to the person who knows what is going on in your head.

Are you tasting the mystery of being with God? Then the answers are already near you. Day by day, God's plan will become clearer. You will have the vision that fulfills God's desire rather than the dream of achieving your own goals. Of course, that is a strictly personal answer that God will grant to you. Not the God of renowned pastors or faithful elders but meet the God that is with you through all your sincere albeit fumbling, flustered ramblings, and gives you His Word. Try concentrating on Him. This is the very start of answers.

Now you know the content, then what should you pray for?

"Pastor, how do you pray?"

Many teenagers and college students ask me this. Every summer we have a great festival for the youth and college students. Even in the leaders meeting prior to the festival, this question invariably turns up. Although pleased by the students' interest in my prayer topics and habits, I also sense that they are struggling quite a bit with the concept of "prayer." Let me address a few points in hopes that it will help many young people unravel their misconceptions regarding prayer.

Although I have raced through the past 30 years thinking solely of evangelism, I have only sensed that my life has been amidst answers to prayer for the past 20 years. Even while evangelizing in the field and lecturing in front of people, I struggled with the difficulty of prayer for quite some time. So my point is that there is no need to be discouraged just because prayer does not come to you as easily as you thought it would.

In order to lecture to people who evangelize in the field or have a passion for evangelism, I had no choice but to pray before God. My mind and body became accustomed to prayer as I experienced the spiritual strength and wisdom which God supplied. The message relayed during Sunday worship or at the conferences were not made overnight but came together over a long period of time. They did not come pouring out all off a sudden one day. I came to realize that this was prepared by God for a long time and only after a long time had passed did I realize that this was God's far-reaching and deliberate plan.

If there is anything that has changed for me after realizing prayer, it is that I can see God's plan more immediately, moment by moment. Frankly speaking, there were many times, where I found myself saying, "Ah, so that's what it was" after everything had all ready taken place. However, from the moment I began to enjoy the God who controls my entire life, moment by moment, I could uncover the plan and direction God desired.

Begin this way

Look up and read Psalm chapter 1. You can infer from

the words that the surest and safest way to begin prayer is with meditation on the Word. It is greatly beneficial to get into the habit of beginning your day by meditating on the Word. Honestly, prayer begins from the moment you meditate on the Word, the letter, which contains God's mysteries. You will enjoy true peace in your heart and gain assurance in your heart which you could not receive from anyone, anywhere, when you deeply meditate on the Word.

A college student studying abroad in Germany said that he was lonely and felt like he was withering away off by himself in a foreign place. However, attending a retreat during a brief visit to Korea during vacation truly strengthened him. When he returned to Germany, he got up early in the morning to either watch the video of the Sunday service or to listen to the message and prayed. An amazing thing occurred. Whereas in the past, he was barely able to keep up with his studies and always struggling with loneliness being away from his family, he now gained a sense of confidence and joyfully passed each day filled with strength.

If you believe that this kind of transformation is only for special people, that is a grave misconception. We can discuss this once you have tried meditating on the Word every morning. You will realize how refreshing and exhilarating it is to start each day with the strength that God gives. I am not saying you merely feel good. As you pray, your prayer topics amazingly become more organized and clearer. When the Word is fulfilled in your life, you will find yourself naturally taking an interest in evangelism. By the time you sense, "Wow, God is with me and He is leading me!" others will have noticed it as well. They will say, "Ah, God must be with that person!" The "filling of the Holy Spirit" you so long for is this.

Just remember two things. If you want to go to a prayer retreat center or to some solitary place to pray, you really need to convince yourself to take the first step to get there. That is why, there is no better method than to pray day by day to receive daily answers. If you are in the habit of seeking out someone to gain comfort and strength when things get hard, then get rid of that. Throughout the week, call to mind the message God gave you during Sunday worship and gain strength first on your own. If you are living the walk of faith where someone always needs to hold your hand then you will only receive answers at the level of a newborn or pampered child. If you gain the strength that God gives on your own every day, then you already possess the mystery of prayer.

From that perspective, prayer is your lifestyle

According to the statistics, only 20% of people between the ages of 15 and 65 living in South Korea are satisfied with how they spend their leisure time. The rest of the 80% are not satisfied with how they spend their leisure time and the percentage is especially low for those between the ages of 30 to 39. The fact that most people in their 30's are immersed in their careers is probably reflected in that figure.

What are you like when you are alone? How different is the you that studies at school and hangs out with friends from the you that sits alone in your room? Pressured by your office superiors, sweating away the hours working with your business colleagues, plodding wearily home from work, coming home and facing your children, how do you rate yourself? Being able to adapt to your surroundings and circumstances is a healthy attitude but the dissociation we have between our social life and spiritual walk of faith can make us develop an inconsistent self image.

Without a doubt we, who have realized the Gospel, are needed in this world. However, in school, at work, and as we run our businesses, it is amazing how often we forget how important and influential we are.

Prayer = lifestyle

When prayer is established in our lifestyle and our lifestyle is established in prayer, the quality of our walk of faith will be better and more grace-filled than it is right now. The deeper we enjoy the mystery of prayer, the more we uncover God's will in all circumstances and receive God's guidance. That is why the phrase that comes to mind is "establish prayer in your lifestyle." Then how can we establish prayer in our lifestyle? Rather than rattling off prayer topics, we must enjoy the principal source of prayer first. Enjoying Immanuel is the beginning of prayer. Proverbs 1:7 states, "The fear of the Lord is the beginning of knowledge." Knowing God, being with God is the principal source, the root of our lives. It may seem obvious but there is something different about the people who enjoy Immanuel.

Enjoy your God-given status and authority. This is the

content of prayer. Just as important as enjoying the blessings God has already given you, is to enjoy the things God will grant in the future. God has prepared answers in the place where you are right now. God will give proof through the work you are doing and the part you are entrusted with.

If I were to pinpoint the most important thing regarding prayer, it would be the prayer you pray by yourself. We do need to attend prayer meetings and pray together with others but the prayer we pray by ourselves is more important. A person's life changes depending on how much he enjoys the mystery of prayer in his time alone. When you set aside a time to pray not only does God answer what you ask for but He fulfills His will and works everything according to His sovereignty.

Setting aside a time to pray means that you are orienting your lives around prayer. God works and operates during the time you pray. A bag of money will probably not drop from heaven and your fields will not have magically changed. However, as you pray, you will see that the place where you are standing has changed. It will have changed into a place of blessings and answers. Although he was sold as a slave and sent to prison, Joseph never lost hold of the blessing of prayer and he always stood atop the place of blessings. Not only did he stand before

Pharaoh, he rose to govern the world.

Then, what is the reason we must pray continuously? Our way of thinking and emotions change moment by moment. If we do not pray continuously, we can make incorrect judgments and decisions, or get swept up by our emotions and not see what is truly important. The world we live in is also changing moment by moment. We may face hardships because of an unexpected event. Who can understand the things that go through our hearts? That is why we need the prayer of looking to God.

"All because we do not carry, everything to God in prayer."

These lyrics are from a hymn. What do they mean? It expresses the writer's frustration over the fact that answers are bound to come if we pray, but still people do not pray. What are people who do not know prayer like? Either they are barely able to make a living, unable to sleep from the burdens of their hearts constricting their chests, facing grave illnesses, entangled in serious problems, or more or less just getting by. They do not know why they need to pray and go about their lives unable to fathom the answers that would come if they did pray. They have become accustomed to this vicious cycle of living.

There is a fitting saying that those who have tasted beef know how to eat it well. When you pray, you receive answers.

After receiving answers, you get a taste of prayer. Those who have gotten a taste of this, pray again. This is the good cycle. Therefore, you realize that everything is inside of prayer and that prayer is the amazing key to wielding the name of Jesus Christ.

You must communicate to know

There are many women whose hands are cold even in the middle of summer. There are various reasons why their hands and feet are cold such as, lack of exercise or their nature but the main culprit is poor circulation. The blood circulates when the heart constricts. The blood transports oxygen, carbon dioxide and various other nutrients and toxins. Poor circulation can be the root reason for many diseases because cells do not receive the necessary oxygen and nutrients.

The walk of faith is the same. Just as the blood moves around every corner of the body, the person who constantly communicates with God has abundant nutrients transported to their soul, mind, and life. Their spiritual strength does not wane, they have sincere joy, and they live a healthy and worthwhile life.

What exactly does it mean to connect with God? Without

hesitation, shout "okay" to the following questions.

Answer honestly; do you believe in God's power?

God blesses you every time you come before Him. God wants to listen to your prayers and always wants to give you good things.Hebrews 11:6 He wants to give His children new grace every day.Hebrews 4:6 When you draw near to God, He wants you to race to him bursting with joy and delight. When you believe that God has prepared the very best thing for you, you can pray and God looks for that sincere, child-like faith.

At times, you may become disappointed or disheartened. You may face situations that drive you to your knees. When your heart becomes diseased, you grow weak physically and your health deteriorates. At that moment, evil forces can gain a foothold. But remember! God wants to give new grace every day. Simply go before God just as you are with nothing to hide. God is more than able to save you. The issue is do you believe that?

Let me ask another question, do you believe the Word?

God's Word is definitely living and active even now, so works absolutely arise when you hear the Word, place the Word in your heart, and pray. God's ways are truly amazing and mystical. And one of those is the power of the Word. From the past until today,

God moved the world through the Word and He worked and even now works through those who hold to that Word. Finding God's will through the words of the Sunday worship, through daily meditation on the Word is the blessing God's children must enjoy. Do you believe the words God has given to you?

If so, then you are a person of faith

People have their own standards and expectations for making decisions. They take in their surroundings and make judgment calls based on their past experiences or acquired knowledge anticipating certain outcomes. However, within this process there can be prejudices and biases.

Faith is the vessel. Mark 11:24 records, "Therefore I tell you, whatever you ask in prayer, believe that you have received it, and it will be yours." What does this mean? Will you stubbornly continue to hold to your standards and shallow knowledge in front of God? No one can estimate what God is planning or how He will bring about that plan. However, the sure thing is that God does not want us to perish or fail. That is why your vessel is important. If you align your thoughts and vessel to God, works that could not possibly be done by your strength will arise.

Countless thoughts cross your mind every day. You may

be satisfied with your work and feel a sense of accomplishment and then there are times when you have no clue where you are heading. Anyway, you reassure yourself that there is no such thing as failure for God's child then turn around to become ensnared by pessimistic thoughts wondering why you have no special talents, or no great background with no ray of hope in sight.

Think back on why you are living today. Are you living to lift up the name of Jesus Christ and proclaim the Gospel or are you perhaps using the Gospel to carry out your own agenda? If you find that your sincere heart for the Gospel has grown faint, stop beating yourself over it and set it right again.

If you align your life to the Gospel day by day, your life will ultimately be a life that connects with God, and you are well on your way to fulfilling God's will. As proof of this, God will give you peace deep within your heart.

Prayer can do all things

You know that Jesus is the Christ but have you ever felt that something was lacking in your life? The world renowned author C.S. Lewis expressed it this way.

"A car is made to run on petrol, and it would not run properly on anything else. Now God designed the human machine to run on Himself. He Himself is the fuel our spirits were designed to burn, or the food our spirits were designed to feed on. There is no other way."

There is no relationship in this world, no matter how intimate, that is as needed and important as our relationship with God. Therefore, as much as you maintain your relationship with God, you gain strength to live and find meaning in changing your field. No matter how great of a car you possess, you need gasoline if you want to start the engine and go for a spin.

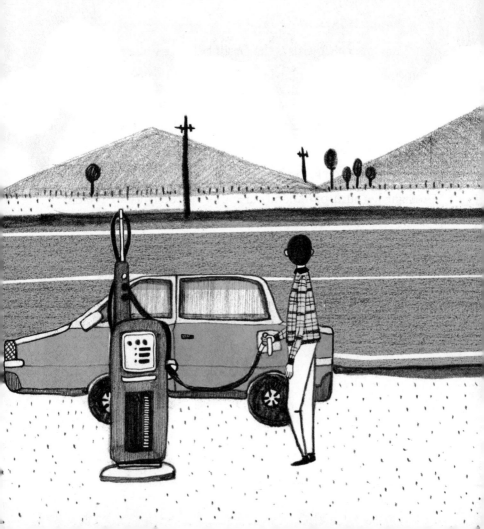

Regardless of performance or fuel efficiency, cars need gasoline to run properly. That is how they are made. People must meet God and trust in Him in order to live the proper life. That is how we are created. Therefore, there is nothing more important or necessary than our relationship with God. God who created you, is with you and guides you. It is like being guaranteed gasoline to fuel our car for the rest of our lives.

Reflect on whether you have the following five assurances and check your fuel gauge.

Confirm whether you have the status that has received salvation, has become a child of God, and will never perish. God will never allow us to come to the dead end of failure. We had no choice but to live under the influence of the forces of darkness, filled with suffering and agony, and ultimately go to hell, but now we have been delivered from sin and curses and are free. This is the very reason Jesus Christ, God's Son, came to this earth. Even though they have already been set free, there are some people who forget that fact and live like they are not free at all. Satan will continue to attack them. He will make them worry, fill their hearts with burdens, and make them live in fear.

Think about the fact that Jesus Christ bore all of our sins in your place. Do you know about "special pardons?" A special pardon is when the president grants clemency to certain criminals and they no longer need to carry out their sentence. What we have received is no different. Jesus Christ resolved all the past mistakes and shameful sins we want to keep hidden. The worries that follow you around and leave you breathing out sigh after sigh, the diseases and problems which seem to have no solution, all these are no longer yours. However, why does it seem as if you are constantly surrounded by worries and problems? God's amazing plan and mystical ways are hidden there.

God only gives us trials we can handle. There may be many times when you become discouraged and disappointed by the immediate problems before you. However, God's view and God's thoughts are definitely different from ours. If you have realized the Gospel, then you will never face ultimate destruction or failure. Do you feel like giving up because of your limitations or inner scars? Do you feel helpless before the problems, which seem as immovable as mountains? Are you being persecuted because of the Gospel?

God is with us and guiding us. This promise that He is with us is like being guaranteed gas to fuel our car for the rest of our lives. God said to ask for whatever you want. What does this mean? Don't you feel of sense of confidence? The one who can do all things, who can grant all things is interested in you and asking you this question. He wants to know what you want.

Begin praying starting today. Know, remember, and enjoy the fact that when you pray God sends His heavenly army and God's kingdom comes. Someone once said that prayer is like breathing. Together with the biological process of breathing in oxygen and breathing out carbon dioxide, do spiritual breathing.

The earnest prayer of wrestling with God with all your might, there is no way God will not listen to that prayer, there is no way He will not answer with the best thing. Armed with the power of God who moves the world, live your life day by day with peace and answers. Be thankful that you can pray 24 hours a day and fully taste the joy of prayer. There is no happier person or more satisfying life than this.

Do you know
the heart of a parent?

If a friend comes calling at night saying he is hungry, there is not anyone who will pull the bed covers over their head and go back to sleep because he does not want to be disturbed. You will not be able to turn him away because he is your friend but also because you will not be able to ignore his earnest request. Even if you do not have much to eat, you will open the refrigerator door and hand him something.

• Luke 11:13
If you then, who are evil,
know how to give good gifts to your children
how much more will the heavenly Father
give the Holy Spirit to those who ask him!

You just fell into a deep sleep when the doorbell rings.
You are a bit annoyed but you scratch your head
and make your way to the video intercom.

It is well past midnight.
Pacing in front of your friend's house now for over three hours.
You think about leaving but have nowhere particular to go,
but you cannot muster up the nerve to knock on your friend's door.

God is almighty, and we are the children of that Almighty God. If we do not receive answers to prayer, it would be illogical. What parent would give their child a snake when he asks for meat, or give him a scorpion when he asks for an egg? Moreover, there is no way God will not give the Holy Spirit to His children who ask for it. Therefore, it is rightful for the Holy Spirit to work when God's child prays.

The Israelites entering Canaan was the rightful event that God promised. However, the Red Sea was clearly standing in their way. We have all probably experienced such things as well. We acted believing that it was God's will, but instead of smoothly working out, it becomes more complicated and frustrating. Should you become discouraged and resentful at this time? However, there are many times when situations like these give rise to God's miracles. It was like that in the Bible and in our present reality as well. It if is God's plan, He can grant unlimited wisdom to dim-witted fools, and He can provide a way to escape even when there seems to be no way out.

To put it plainly, "prayer is a science." We may not be able to see it with our eyes, but a series of events happen when we pray. When we pray, change absolutely arises in the spiritual realms. The moment we pray in faith, the Holy Spirit works. If the Holy

50   Experience God's love through Small Prayer

Spirit works, the forces of darkness loss their strength and run away. When you pray while studying at your desk or working in your office, God fulfills His Word through His angels and works according to His will. Works arise when we believe. God knows all too well whether we possess faith or not. And it just so happens that Satan knows this as well.

After realizing the Gospel, I unceasingly experienced the God who answers prayers. I believed in God but was still poor, and rather than tasting grace within that poverty, I was more inclined to worry and despair. I had misgivings whether God truly existed and whether Christians could truly show their class and worth in this competitive society filled with seemingly outstanding people.

As I came to understand the Gospel, my faith also grew. I did not suddenly find a strong background or become a millionaire overnight but the hesitation and anxiety disappeared and I gained the assurance that if it is by God's power then nothing would be too hard. By grace, from that point on, I was able to live my life proclaiming the Gospel and truly see the establishment of the people and system to evangelize the entire world coming to realization before my very eyes.

A parent's heart holds unending love as well as sympathy for a child. We consider the ideal parents as the ones who look after their children with eyes full of love and concern, who turn their ears to even the smallest cries, who teach them the tools they will need in life, and directs them to the good path.

Restore your thanksgiving now, for we have a father God who knows what we need before we even ask and answers us the moment we pray as if He was just waiting for us to ask. Given the prior condition that the father God listens to the prayers of His children, we would be doing wrong by God if we become discouraged or worried.

Your prayer right now, is the real you

What kind of prayers are you praying these days? If prayer is distant from your life, let me phrase this question a bit differently. What do you think about the most these days? What do you want to do most when you are by yourself? What is the first thing that comes to mind when you are all alone with no one to disturb you? That may be what is imprinted in your mind and soul.

Do you understand the Gospel?

There are many times that children amaze you as they grow up. A young child, who cannot yet speak, begins to understand words; their vocabulary increasing day by day as their brains develop. They ask questions when they do not understand something. They are intelligent to the point where they will even correct adults if they catch them saying something incorrect.

Children mature through diverse experiences. The Gospel we have received is far greater than this process. Everything is inside the Gospel. Unending answers come to those who understand the Gospel. This is because there is life inside of them.

Even if you are facing a problem, if you have the Gospel it will not be that great of a problem. Even if you do not have any problems in your life, if you do not have the Gospel, that itself will be a problem. What is the use if you have the latest smart phone? Only when you are connected with a service provider, make calls and use various applications does that smart phone truly become "smart." The same goes for us. Only when our spirits meet God, fellowship and communicate with God can we find the true meaning in being human.

What is the Gospel-nature?

The expression 'Gospel nature' is unfamiliar to many people. Enjoying the Gospel, means that the Gospel is evident in our lifestyle and is the very basis of our lives, just like the character you are born with. Simply put, the person with the Gospel nature is the one who has joy and thanksgiving in the Gospel wherever he goes, whatever he faces, and whomever he meets. How you form a Gospel nature is a very personal process, but if you do not have a Gospel nature, it will be difficult to escape from your weaknesses, the life patterns that bring repetitive failure, and the habits that hold you back, even though you are a child of God.

Peter gave the amazing confession, "Jesus is the Christ, the Son of the Living God," but afterwards, he denied Jesus. He realized the Gospel, but his nature was not Gospel oriented. However, after meeting the resurrected Jesus Christ, the Gospel gradually began to lead his life and he spent the rest of his life as an evangelist boldly testifying the Gospel.

If you meet various people, you realize that the perspective of those who realize the Gospel and those who do not are quite different. They make vastly different decisions and choices in their lives and in their relationship with others. How they work in whatever organization they are affiliated with and how they serve the church speaks for itself; every move they make is different.

Answer to prayer all lined up in a row

Answers to prayer line up for the person who knows the Gospel and has a Gospel-nature. The Word you received through worship, the realizations you came to during evangelism training all start to become your own. This is because God shows you which way you must go through His Word every time you worship.

Do you think you have to fight desperately with unbelievers and win? Even though you possess the spiritual mystery to overcome the people who do not know God, are you still lost in powerlessness? Even if all the distinguished intellectuals, powerful millionaires, and politicians put their strength together they cannot change God's power at all. Now, pray for the filling of the Holy Spirit each time you worship. God absolutely answers that prayer.

Ask yourself, "What does God want from me, right now?" every morning, throughout the day. Make time to meditate on God's historic request. Align and fix your life, your sight, on God. There is no greater start than this.

Are you living
as an ugly duckling?

A family of ducks were peacefully living by the river. Among them was a different looking duckling. The other ducks floated along on the water, but this duckling could barely stay afloat. He looked and acted differently from the others, and the others treated him harshly. All the other ducks called him, "ugly duckling." The ugly duckling passed each day in sorrow until, one day, he saw a flock of beautiful swans fly by. The ducks that passed their time floating on the water, looked up at the swans enviously. They were so beautiful. However, the ugly duckling looked a lot like the swans. That is when the ugly duckling realized his identity and spread his wings.

We have received salvation but we do not properly live our walk of faith. We try to live our social life honestly, avoiding things that would go against our conscience so there is no way we can keep up with the unbelievers who use every means to succeed. Unaware of the strength that God gives, we lead ambiguous lives unable to either openly reveal that we are God's children or use flattery and cheating to get ahead in life. We complain that we cannot stay afloat like the others and resent the fact that we do not look like the other ducks. Then at least now, let's start correctly living our marvelous lives. God does not exist only in the Bible. Even now, He wants to be with us through the Word, through the name of Christ, and through the Holy Spirit.

The Father God who is with us through the Word

Even now, God is guiding everything through His Word. The method by which the invisible God is with us, is through His Word. Hold to the Word He gives you everyday. What is the Word? The Word is God.John 1:1 He created the universe with the Word.Genesis 1:1-31 God's Word is living and active, piercing to the division of soul and of sprit, of joints and of marrow.Hebrews 4:12 God speaks and acts according to His Word.Genesis 18:19, Jeremiah 33:2 He sends His angels to carry out His Word.Psalm 103:20-22 Hold to even one sentence of the Word God gives you during worship on the Lord's Day and pray for faith to see God's Word work in your life throughout the next six days of the week. God works when we believe in the fulfillment of His Word.

The authority of Jesus Christ's name

I know a certain senior deaconess who exclaims, "O, Lord" every time something slips from her hands or she forgets to do something and suddenly remembers what it was. Many people cry out, "O Lord" without much thought to how powerful those words are. There are not that many people who realistically know the power of that name. If you know the power of the name of Jesus Christ, you have no reason to resent others or complain about your circumstances. We can break down all the forces of Satan and darkness that draw near to us in the name of Jesus Christ. Are you powerless or lethargic? Break that down in the name of Jesus Christ. How great is the name of Jesus Christ? All things are subject to that name.Philippians 3:21 Every knee in heaven and on earth bow to that name.Philippians 2:10 Each time you do scheduled prayer, proclaim, "In the name of Jesus Christ of Nazareth, may all the forces of spiritual ignorance depart!"

The Work of the Holy Spirit

God is with us even now through the Holy Spirit. That is why He told us to be filled by only the Holy Spirit. What is the first thing to being filled by the Holy Spirit? It is opening your spiritual eyes. 1 Corinthians chapter 3 states that people of the flesh are as infants. We do not give a hunk of meat to an infant who cannot even stand. We give the infant what he can eat, milk. If we are people of the flesh with infantile faith, God will not give us the filling of the Holy Spirit. When we become spiritual people, He gives us the power of the Holy Spirit.[John 6:33] When Joseph was sold into slavery, when he was falsely accused and sent to prison, he did not hold a grudge against anyone. He knew God's sovereignty that desired to save lives.

God is living and working even now. He is with us through the Word, through the name of Jesus Christ, and through the Holy Spirit. All you have to do for your walk of faith is simply enjoy the evidence of Immanuel that is already upon you. Simply spread your swan wings. Do not walk around in trepidation, being ridiculed by others, unbefitting your status as a swan. Spread wide you swan wings and beautifully take to the skies.

How to live in this crazy world

A young man went to see Dr. Norman Vincent Peale because of all the problems he was having. Dr. Peale said, "I know a place where there are 100,000 people and not one has a problem." When the young man excitedly said he wanted to go there, Dr. Peale answered, "Okay, I'll give you directions to Woodlawn cemetery!"

Dr. Peale wanted to point out to the young man that there is no place on earth that is free from problems. However, we see many Christians praying to God to take away the hardships and problems they are facing. Jesus taught us to pray, "and lead us not into temptation." This means that as we live in this world, there are many temptations and many problems. Then how can we receive answers to prayer amidst the hardships and problem?

Gain wisdom from the problem

Psalm 119 contains the confession of a believer facing hardships.

• Psalm 119:28
My soul melts away for sorrow;
strengthen me according to your word!

• Psalm 119:61
Though the cords of the wicked ensnare me,
I do not forget your law.

• Psalm 119:69
The insolent smear me with lies,
but with my whole heart I keep your precepts.

• Psalm 119:143
Trouble and anguish have found me out,
but your commandments are my delight.

• Psalm 119:176
I have gone astray like a lost sheep;
seek your servant, for I do not forget your commandments

Of course, you will face problems in life. In one sense, they are inevitable. Incidents that make your heart jump explode all around you, at times you are the victim of misunderstandings, and then again, you become the one guilty of slander as you greedily try to add one more thing to your pile. There are times when it is your fault the problem becomes full blown and then there are times when you face a problem and have no idea where it came from. Your family or someone close to you can suddenly become sick or you find yourself drowning in debt.

However, rather than external pressures that come from your surroundings or circumstances, the more serious problem is when you lose your identity. When this happens, you get caught up in problems completely forgetting who you are and flail helplessly in grief and despair. You feel like there is nothing you can do, life has passed you by, and the future looks bleak. Doing your best and living honestly seem futile. What can you do?

The problem needs to be resolved but it can be the opportunity to gain God's wisdom. No matter what kind of hardship you are in, simply receive grace through God's Word. No matter where you are, no matter what circumstances you find yourself in, there is no reason to fear or worry. God is keeping watch over you and protecting you. No matter how evil the world may appear, just do not stumble and fall into the problem.

"Why is my family so poor? Why are my parents so

powerless? Why was I born into this family? What's wrong with my husband, my wife?" No matter how many questions you ask, it will not solve the problem. A person lost in these kinds of worries is pressured by his circumstances and has no choice but to despair and lose to that situation. "Even though I am born into this kind of family, I will not lose to hardship." Have this kind of faith.

Are you surrounded by problems? Is someone making your life difficult? 2 Timothy chapter 3 states that there will be times of difficulty in the last days and it will be a time of spiritual confusion where people do not believe in God. Even though the world is wicked and confusing, it is not wise to always look at the world from a negative point of view. There is also no reason to become discouraged, shaken, or taken aback by the world either.

Who am I and where is here

Just because the majority of people mistakenly use their unawareness of God to cry out that God does not exist, does not mean that He actually does not exist. However, you need something to back you up in order to proclaim that He exists when the entire world says that He does not. It is not about obstinance or tenacity but assurance and proof.

What must God's child do?

Know who you are. It is important to not stumble and fall into problems but it is more important to know who you are. The people who believe that Jesus is the Christ are clearly the saved children of God. God's children can find out who they are when they listen to God's Word, when they meditate on the Word. People who are about to enter a prestigious university must go knowing who they are. Those who know who they are as they study, work, or raise their children, will have a different start, process, and outcome.

Answer to prayer begins with knowing who you are. You are a saved child of God. God sent Jesus Christ to this earth to save you and bought you by His blood. Where are you living and what are you doing right now? If you are a student, then as a student; if you are a soldier, then as a soldier; if you are a congressmen, then as a congressman; live in a manner that befits who you are. Overestimating yourself and becoming arrogant or underestimating yourself and becoming discouraged means that you do not know yourself well. Do you really know who you are?

No matter what kind of hardship comes or how great things are, if you know who you are, you will not be shaken. God's children never fail.

The person who truly understands himself,
has no choice but to be thankful.

The person who knows how weak, lacking and even wicked he can be at times has no choice but to lay himself down before God.

The more you know yourself, the more you will cling to God.

Chapter 02

Renowned
life

You come home, wash up.
Your heart and body begin to relax.

You put on comfortable clothes
and it feels good to spend time
thinking about this and that.

You can reflect on grand things like
your life's direction or goals.
Or spend time thinking about more realistic
things like the work you did today
or what you will say
to the people you will meet tomorrow.

Sit back and close your eyes.
The greatest joy
lies in this time of prayer.

Are they truly renowned people?

The one who has renowned thoughts is the renowned person. A person's life is forged depending on what their thoughts are and what they have set their heart on. They will receive answers to the extent of how big and wide the vessel of their hearts and minds is. Your thoughts must be deep and cool while your heart must be aflame with passion. The heart must be simple and clear to keep from wavering but the mind must be systematic and broad. To begin with the conclusion, the person who prays is the renowned individual. This is because God guards your heart and mind when you pray.Philippians 4:7

Do not say a word if you do not know
what blessings you have received
Praying without knowing the blessing inside of Christ is as

futile as asking a preschooler about policy issues. The blessings God's children have received can largely be divided into status and authority.

First, pray the pray of enjoying your God-given status. Since the Holy Spirit dwells in the hearts of God's children, God's light shines wherever they go and the forces of darkness flee. God has chosen you and called you a royal priesthood, a holy nation, a people for His own possession.[1 Peter 2:9] That is why you have a reason to proclaim the excellencies of Him who called you out of darkness into His marvelous light. You need strength to live in this world. Pray so that the Holy Spirit will work everywhere you go. You will gain the strength to transcend that you will not be able to gain anywhere else in this world.

Second, pray the prayer of enjoying your God-given authority. If you look in Revelations 8:3-5, it records that angels carry the prayers of the believers in censers up before the throne of God. Of course, we cannot see angels, but God's Word is living and active; it will absolutely be fulfilled. So those who believe this fact will definitely pray. You can also break Satan's forces in Jesus Christ's name. Heaven is rightfully guaranteed for God's children when they die but they can still enjoy the kingdom of God where they are right now. The hymn that confesses "Where Jesus is, 'tis heaven there" is prayer.

The content and form of prayer is absolutely not rigid

The prayer known as the "Lord's Prayer" is the prayer Jesus taught his disciples during his earthly ministry. The Lord's Prayer begins, "Our father in heaven." The Greek word for heaven "οὐρανος," contains the meaning "the sky" and "the heavens." The God who listens to your prayers is the Almighty God who rules over and governs the entire universe. Only when you acknowledge the condition that He is none other than your father, can you entrust everything to Him. Jesus also taught us to pray this way. "Hallowed be your name. Your kingdom come, your will be done on earth as it is in heaven."

The best way to pray is to comfortably pray in the way that fits you best, in the time that works for you. Another wise method is to designate a time and spend the rest of the day centered on that time. You can also pray as you wash up, as you eat, while riding on the bus, while taking a walk, before or after class. The person that connects everything to prayer moment by moment will give off spiritual leisure and the fragrance of grace. Do you want a life overflowing with answers beyond your expectations? The answer lies in prayer.

The person who knows prayer is the happy person

As you deal and work with many kinds of people, misunderstandings and troublesome problems may arise. To avoid exacerbating the situation, sometimes you keep your emotions hidden, even though you are hurting inside. Sometime, you even lie and say that everything is all right, even though it is not. Everyone wants to have good relations and live a beautiful life. However thinking "Will things get better if I go somewhere else? Will it get better if I meet a good person?" is a waste of time. If you start incorrectly, worrisome things are inevitable.

What does it mean to hold to the Word?

Find what you have lost hold of in your life first. When God reveals the things He has hidden, He often spoke in parables. However, no matter how much He speaks in parables, there are people who simply do not realize. These kind of people are deceived every time things become difficult. Since they do not gain strength from the Word God gives, they go to this person and that person and only turn to God after everything blows up. To hold to the Word means to apply the Word from the Sunday worship and the Word you received in your everyday life to every aspect of your life. There are quite a few people who press the "delete" key and discard the Word they received in the trash bin of their brains or file away the Word in a folder they can never find again as they return from church. If you hold to the Word, it will permeate into your real life such as your work, your child rearing, PTA meetings, school life, relationships, dating, marriage, entrance exams, job hunting…etc. Time and again you will realize, "This is what the Words God gave to me mean; this is God's plan." It will be the mystery by which you connect with God.

When nothing works out

Do things always work out the way you planned? There are times you tried to do your best but it still did not work out. You may often think, "Why doesn't anything work out for me? You feel nervous no matter what you choose; you become hesitant no matter what you do. You find yourself talking more but not having any clear answer; the only thing that seems to be increasing is you critical judgment of others.

If you have not done anything that wrong and tried just as hard as the next guy, but still feel as if your life has not amounted to much, then that is a problem that needs to be addressed. On a recent talk show, a famous celebrity brought up this topic. No matter how much wealth he acquired, how much love and affection he received from people, no matter how much glory and fame he achieved, and how many good and charitable deeds he did, he realized that there is a certain percentage of his life that is still empty. It takes insight and wisdom to realize that.

People must be with God in order to ultimately fill that empty space. From the moment humankind was tempted by Satan and separated from God, they cannot have sincere happiness no matter what or how hard they try. There is no way humankind can find happiness as they live their lives studying, working, dating, marrying, and rearing children under the hand of Satan whose very reason for being is to destroy mankind. God sent Jesus to solve this problem. Jesus died and resurrected to solve life's problem of suffering, pain, and emptiness. Whoever believes Jesus as the Lord and savior of their life will be changed.

A new life unfolds. The reason is that from that moment on, the God who created you is with you. This is the Gospel.

Can you comprehend the Christ who solved all the problems? Is Jesus Christ the answer for your family? Do you have the mystery of God being with you in your life? If not, you are diligently living your life but going in the wrong direction. Break your foolish pride. The thoughts and habits you simply cannot discard even though you know that they are deceiving you, make the bold decision to say good-bye to them. If you gain the strength that God gives, nothing can be a problem. When you enjoy the mystery of God being with you, even though you may not be able to change the events and circumstances, you will be able to nimbly change your thoughts and attitude.

No matter where you are,
in that very place

"The school and workplace you belong to is your God-given mission field."

How does your heart feel as you read that sentence? Do you gladly respond, "That's right, the God who saved me has sent me to this place right now." Or does it make you sigh, "This frustrating, complicated, problem-filled place is my mission field?

If you look at Acts 1:1, Luke writes, "In the first book, O Theophilus." The grace and works of God that Luke, who realized the Gospel, recorded for Theophilus not only saved that one person but also influenced that entire age. The words of the Gospel, which you gave, will not only strengthen and comfort someone but also save lives.

The school, company, and workplace where you are is the mission field; this means that you are the missionary there, then

Life is often difficult and exhausting.
You want every day to be fun and worthwhile,
But caught up in the rat race of your everyday life,
you mindlessly go to work, school, and live day by day.
Answers do not come from a distant place unfolding
like a grand event.
You receive them, one by one,
through your ordinary, everyday life.

how will you enjoy this amazing answer?

If you have this first, the rest will follow

I am speaking of faith and skill. Joseph and David enjoyed in their average day the fact that God was with them and gave their confession of faith in the place where they were. Furthermore, they had integrity and skill in whatever they were entrusted with. Begin your day with faith in one hand and your studies or work in the other. This kind of person will succeed no matter where he is placed. Are you in the habit of just adequately passing the time until you get off from school or work? This is because you do not believe what you are doing is worth anything more than that. The person who knows the importance of his place and worth will definitely put in the effort.

We are prone to make resolutions and see them quickly fade away. We make plans thinking that nothing will get in our way but in actually carrying them out, it is natural for us to hit a few difficulties along the way. That is why we need the tenacity to see things through to the end and not become discouraged. As well as continuously asking and seeking to find God's hidden plan.

All students study and all company workers do their job. However, while some students have a clear goal and pour all their interest into their national ranking, others cannot wait for the testing period to end. Those who have a vision have the goal of racing towards uniqueness; that is why something about them is different.

Enjoy always

Find a way to enjoy studying. Find a way to enjoy your work. No matter how hard a person works, they cannot overtake the one who enjoys what he is doing. Do you resent the fact that you are the only one studying while everyone else is sleeping or you are the only one working while all your coworkers are out drinking? How precious is that time; have the wisdom to know the great works that will arise because of that time.

Especially when problems come, wait for the answers that are right behind that problem. Just know that right now you are marching along the path that God wants the most. Then begin with a change of heart. The more you work, the more you study, the more strength you will gain.

It is rightful for those who need help to seek out those who can help

What is the image people bring to mind when they think of

you? Are you a person who is laid back and trustworthy enough for people to want to come to for help? If you look carefully at people who talk a lot and crave attention, you will often see that they lack substance. The person who truly helps another to the very end is the genuine friend. The one who is truly skilled is the person who quickly analyzes what is needed in that place and situation and knows how to meet that need. Simply put, just stay one step ahead of the person next to you and realistically work harder than all the others.

How can you do that? It would be difficult by our strength or power, but it is possible by God's spirit.Zechariah 4:6 If you receive the filling of the Holy Spirit, you will see the things of the future,Joel 2:28 and God will pour down evidence so that you can stand as His witness to the ends of the earth.Acts 1:8

Gain the strength that God gives and arise. Pull yourself together and clearly remember that you are a missionary. Then being acknowledged as "a truly classy person" in the place where you are will only be a matter of time.

What does evangelism have to do with answered prayer

What is world like right now?

God showed us in advance the things that would take place in the world during the end times. If you look at Matthew chapter 24, the things that will happen are recorded in detail. Matthew 24:14 states, "And this gospel of the kingdom will be proclaimed throughout the whole world as a testimony to all nations, and then the end will come." 2 Timothy 3:1~17 states that there will be times of difficulty in the last days and there too the events are recorded in detail. Also in 2 Timothy chapter 4 it says, "preach the word; be ready in season and out of season."

The bible references in several places that there will be spiritual confusion in the future. Then as someone who has received the Gospel, how should you accept this world?

The other side of evangelism

As you go to the evangelism field, you realize God's plan. As you go to the evangelism field, your prayer topics become organized. As you evangelize, you come to realize, "Wow, the Word is living and active!" Find the answer to all the problems in the field and just uncover the answers hidden inside the problem.

God's desire is for every person to hear the Gospel and receive salvation. If you live embracing God's desire but your life is a mess and your heart is not at peace, then something must be wrong. We have already been set free from all the problems of our past, present, and future by meeting God. Furthermore, since evangelism is God's composite blessing, it is rightful for God to bless the evangelist's daily life and entire life.

The answer to prayer that comes when you understand evangelism.

When you understand evangelism, answers to prayer comes. The reason being that to say you understand evangelism means you know God's true desire. Make your life resolution to do what God wants the most. Then victory is inevitable. As you think about evangelism, you can see God's desire, as well as His plan and vision.

Evangelism is the mirror with which to view yourself. Evangelism is the opportunity by which you can confirm your level and training by examining how much you love the Gospel, how much you possess the content for saving lives, and how much your eyes have opened to see the field. Just like looking in a mirror, correctly see your true self. Do not become discouraged or conceited by what you see, just set your heart right again.

Since we are weak, trials and errors are inevitable. However, as you organize your prayer topics one by one inside evangelism, they will become like treasures and shine and you will receive unique answers that are incomparable to anyone else. When you designate a time and pray inside of evangelism, you will see the Word being fulfilled in your life, and experience how all the big and little things that arise inside of evangelism come together to bring about God's will. The Almighty God knows everything, so trust Him and entrust everything to Him, in the very place you are right now.

• 1 Timothy 2:3b~4
God our Savior, who desires all people to be saved
and to come to the knowledge of the truth

The place where you live and your church will be revived

Time is too precious to waste on being discouraged and wandering and when we become this way the blessings and grace we received are put to shame. If you do not receive the strength that God gives, we lose hold of the blessings we must enjoy in the field and barely survive even though we have already gained everything. If you hold to the following things, you will fully triumph amidst the various realities and incidents that try to discourage you.

Unbelief warning!

One of the greatest ways to overcome unbelief is found in 1 Thessalonians 5:16~18, "Rejoice always, pray without ceasing, give thanks in all circumstances." Satan plows into our hearts and souls by planting thoughts of unbelief. Pray as if you are conversing with God. It will be difficult to receive answers if you have lost hold of who you are and why you are living. In that state, even if you do get answers, you will not recognize them as answers.

The one who knows his self-identity can always rejoice. The person who has a sense of mission can pray without ceasing, and the person who has a sense of calling can give thanks in all circumstances. Like the words of Romans 8:28, no matter what happens we have the God who works all things together for the good. Then is there any worry that can overtake us?

It is not because you do not know the field

As we live in the fields of your life, we will encounter times when the words we received so graciously during worship, do not seem to match with us anymore. At those times, we can get lost in worries. We do need to be able to look at the field for what it is but there is no reason for us to become frustrated or discouraged as we look at our present reality. This is because there is a door God has prepared for each and every person. God has the best plan for the field we are in, but Satan also shoots arrows of unbelief and deceives us. If we correctly know and enjoy the spiritual facts, then we will see the evidence of our field changing. When we pray, the Holy Spirit works, the Lord's angels carry out His will, and the forces of darkness flee. We may not be able to see this with our eyes, but this really happens and those who receive this answer can never fail.

Do not let anyone or anything steal away your personal prayer time. During that time, uncover what you must do for the rest of your life through your occupation or talent. Organize the prayer topics God gave to you through His daily Word, look back on how you have grown and your present circumstances and you will be able to find your lifelong prayer topics. If you are worrying over a yet unresolved spiritual hardship or habit, or if you have a problem that needs immediate attention just give thanks to God. You can look to God because of that hardship or problem, and since God has called us to save others using that pain as a platform you will be inspired daily by God's in-depth plan.

• 1 Thessalonians 5:16~18
Rejoice always, pray without ceasing,
give thanks in all circumstances;
for this is the will of God in Christ Jesus for you

Give off good vibes

Whether it is the lady standing in front of her open closet complaining she has nothing to wear, the man pouring over the menu wondering what to eat, or the housewife planning what to cook for dinner, the same 24 hours are given to them all. The teenager who rushes off to school tired of hearing his parents nagging him, the employee who wants to say, "I am out of here" and escape from the piles of paper work on his desk, or the CEO who feels the responsibility of running the company weighing heavily on his shoulder; how they spend their 24 hours may be diverse and different but it is still the same 24 hours. They each have their own reasons and circumstances. And there are times we wonder how we need to understand the many people and situations we meet in our lives. Perhaps the breadth of that curiosity may be wider for the person who has received salvation.

This is because we are aware that we do not live their lives by our own will or effort. We may have heard the words "God's sovereignty" countless times, but the difficult situation or unfair accusations facing us just seems to make the future bleak. God has taken care of our past, present, and even future problems but the road we walk seems bleak as if a thick fog is blocking our path. What is even more frustrating is that there is no one you can ask about these kinds of situations.

There is something different about that person

If you are a child of God, confirm your calling everyday. Experience the Jesus who is not your friend's savior, but your savior; not your spouse's savior, but your savior. The saved believer knows who he is and who Christ is, the one who completely solved all the problems. Uncover the "you" that is in the Gospel, find the "you" that is within the works that God is doing, and find the "you" in your present reality. The blessings we have received are too great to resign ourselves to the level of people who only think about, "What should I wear, what should I eat, what should I do."

The people who are a good influence often have a different attitude towards life and they give off a different vibe. They are not interested in pressuring others or trying to persuade people with words. Looking to meet good people is a good thing, but being the good person that others want to meet is pretty classy as well. Then you need to be happier than anyone else, right?

The reason for such joy

The one who personally meets God during worship and eagerly listens for His voice to nourish his soul is truly happy. The reason is that all areas of our lives are restored when we worship and we gain the strength to pull ourselves together. God's child can solve all his life's problems through worship. If you are going to worship, do it to the extent that nothing can be a problem for you. If you can do that, then you will be able to see God's plan. You will see what you need to do and how you should do it. Once you find that, there is no way you will vaguely or recklessly live throughout the day or the week.

The person who has found God's plan for him wants to tell that to the people he meets. Let us say that you mustered up your courage and finally bought the watch or bag that you wanted. Even if you do not say anything directly, the way you strut around will be different from before. This means that those who receive answers will somehow spread that influence to their surroundings.

In one sense, a person in need rightfully looks for someone to help him. Since God's interest is in the salvation of souls, it is rightful that He would send that ready soul to the one who enjoys answers and thinks about how he can share the Gospel. This person cannot become lost in lethargy, depression, or wrath.

The most blessed person on earth is the one who can do what God desires, at the time that God desires. There is nothing sadder than the person who lacks the strength to carry out what God needs at that time, as well as the faith to believe in the God who wants to work through him. If your soul is strengthened by the words you received during worship, and if you spend the week holding to the words that came knocking on the door of your heart, then amazingly you will be able to interpret the things that happen from the perspective of those words and you will be able to confirm the answers. This is answers to prayer. Through the events that unfold, you can see what God will do and what He needs. Those who have seen God's historic request have a joyful and vibrant walk of faith. It is at that time, that meetings with people beyond the confines of your ability and level arise. May you hear God's voice through all your meetings, reflect yourself against the people you meet and learn from them, and live the classy and refreshing life that gives off good vibes.

Renowned people

Choices and decision are very important in life. Most times, actions come at the end of the decision-making process. Even when you apologize, "Oh how thoughtless of me," you actually did think about what kind of attitude and action you must take in that situation. Therefore, what thoughts you have, what you have set your heart on is very important. God promised to guard our hearts and our minds.

• Philippians 4:6~7
Do not be anxious about anything but in everything by prayer
and supplication with thanksgiving let
your requests be made known to God.
And the peace of God, which surpasses all understanding,
will guard your hearts and your minds in Christ Jesus.

When you pray, God gives you the spirit of revelation, enlightens the eyes of your heart, and makes known the riches of his glorious inheritance.Ephesians 1:17-19 During Sunday worship or your personal prayer time, uncover God's plan within His Word! This is the walk of faith.

The Reverend John Calvin said, "Prayer is labor" and in one sense he is correct. However, if prayer is enjoying the fact that God is with me, then rather than hard labor it would be more appropriate to say that prayer is enjoying true peace. When you did not know the mystery of prayer, time spent in prayer may feel hard and tedious. However, if you have resolved your misunderstanding of prayer, then the more you pray, the more the answers will come pouring down. Deep thanksgiving will be restored.

Overstep the problems?

To those who have sincere thanksgiving flowing out of them, problems can no longer be problems. If you believe in the God that sought you out of despair, then you have no choice but to be thankful. This is what a person who enjoys the Gospel looks like. If the words you unwittingly blurt out are filled with resentment and complaints, then that means there is still a myriad of things you do not know about the mystery of the Gospel. When you meditate deeply on and pray over the blessing of salvation you have received, the diseases of your heart are healed, rest and peace come to you, and you even restore your life balance.

Now, put away the life of slander and gossip! Live the life of a witness testifying the answers and evidence you have received. Escape from the envy and jealousy that stem from an inferiority complex and the victim mentality and find God's plan for you. Everyone has scars in their heart. However, whether you remain flailing about in the scars, or turn them into platforms is entirely your choice. Do not be someone who stirs up trouble; be the person who creates a peaceful and stable environment. Break through your legalism and prejudice and be a person who shines with fresh ideas and wisdom.

Where does sincere thanksgiving come from? The person who truly understands himself, has no choice but to be thankful. The person who knows how weak, lacking and even wicked he can be at times has no choice but to lay himself down before God. The more you know yourself, the more you will cling to God. Therefore the person who gives thanks is the truly renowned individual.

It may sound silly,
but we often try to limit God's power
with our brains.

If you lose hold of why God, who makes
no mistakes,
allowed this situation to happen
you will truly be lost in a blind spot.

Chapter 03

The prayers
of the people
in the Bible

How did they pray?

Many parents read stories of great figures to their children. They even invest quite a bit of money to buy entire collections, in hopes that their children will diligently read about the achievements and lives of these great figures and at least try to emulate them.

Renowned individuals and heroes of faith can be found in God's Word, the Bible, as well. It is interesting to see how these people in the Bible learned and enjoyed the prayer we so desire and strive for.

Abraham, his son, and his grandson

Abraham finally received answers once he built an altar to the Lord and began to full-fledge pray.Genesis 13:18 Isaac possessed the mystery of meditative prayer,Genesis 24:63 and Jacob realized

God's covenant as he received the name of "Israel" amidst hardships.^{Genesis 32:22-32} Joseph enjoyed the blessing of God being with him and succeeded wherever he went.^{Genesis 39:1-6} Abraham and Jacob were the type who prayed and received answers each time there was a problem. Isaac and Joseph always prayed in their everyday life. They were different from Abraham and Jacob because they triumphed in prayer whether there were problems or not.

A few people from the Old Testament

Moses realized God's plan at the age of 80. Joshua and Caleb remained steadfast from the very beginning and held to the covenant to the very end.^{Exodus 3:1~20, Joshua 1:1~9, 3:1~12, 6:1~20, 14:6~15} What is more important than fasting or staying awake all night to pray, is laying down the foundation for the habit of praying in your everyday life, from right within your circumstances.

If I had to choose the most outstanding priest, it would be Samuel and the king that received the most answers would be David. Samuel confessed that he would not commit the sin of ceasing to pray and not one word he spoke fell to the ground. While Samuel was alive, wars ceased in Israel and David confessed, "The Lord is my shepherd; I shall not want."^{1 Samuel 3:1~18, Ps 23:1-6}

Look at the outstanding prophets Elijah and Elisha as well as King Hezekiah. Their lives were inside of prayer. God sent His horses and chariots of fire to Elijah and Elisha. God sent His herald and answered the man of prayer, King Hezekiah.2 Kings 2:1~10, 6:8~23, 19:14~35

During the age of captivity, Daniel enjoyed the mystery of prayer and revealed God's existence and power to those who did not know God. Thinking of his people's future, he made a vow, fasted and prayed. God poured down the blessing of making Daniel wiser than all the wisdom of the magicians and enchanters of that age put together.Daniel 2:27~49, 6:10, 10:10~20

Especially Joseph

As you well know, Joseph was sold as a slave to a foreign land at a young age. He did his best in Potiphar's home and gained recognition from his master. No matter what people may say, this verse describes Joseph perfectly, "the Lord was with him and the Lord caused all that he did to succeed in his hands." Enjoying the fact that God was with him was Joseph's top priority. Even when he was wrongfully accused and sent to prison, even when he suddenly became the governor over the land, he unswervingly looked to God.

Amazingly, there is common factor among the people who succeed in their walk of faith. Doing their best in whatever situation they are placed is a given; they entrusted everything, big and small, to God and followed God's will. That is, they prayed. As you live in this world, there are things you can achieve through hard work. There can be things you can gain by relying on people with power, wealth, or people who understand you well. However, you must surely realize by now that there are things in life that simply cannot be done by your strength, no matter how hard you try. Relying on the God who completely knows every situation and circumstance that you cannot even fathom; that was Joseph's prayer.

Hezekiah

There was something Hezekiah did as soon as he became king. He destroyed the idols scattered across the nation and commanded the Israelites to return to the Lord. Furthermore, he ordered that they stop paying tribute since there was no reason to pay taxes to Assyria. Outraged, Assyria invaded with 185,000 soldiers. Invading a country with a population of 15 million with 185,000 soldiers is evident to everyone that they wanted to annihilate the country. Hearing this news, King Hezekiah was

God is alive
whether you acknowledge it or not.
He is everywhere, knows everything,
and can do all thing.
God knows your circumstances,
how you cope,
and the even the state of your heart.
Whatever it is,
lay it down before the God who created you
and has the best scenario for you.

taken aback for a moment. He became anxious and swept up in a whirlwind of worries. Urgently, he sent an envoy conveying his apology and plea for reconciliation. When Assyria executed that envoy, King Hezekiah collected and sent gold, silver, and jewels. He even stripped the gold from the temple and the palace. However, the situation worsened.

Even someone who does well on average can easily be taken aback and flustered in the face of hardships. Hezekiah had faith, but his weaknesses surfaced in the face of problems to the point of making him look quite pitiful. As the 185,000 soldiers laid siege to the city, Hezekiah finally made a resolution. There was nothing more he could do; nothing more he could rely on. He took the declaration of war from Assyria and headed towards the temple. That night, King Hezekiah staked his life and began to pray. He prayed before God with the most earnest and sincere heart. He desperately clung to God. Honestly, he should have done that sooner. That was what God wanted. An amazing thing happened that night. An angel of the Lord appeared and struck down the 185,000 soldiers of the Assyrian army in their own camp. It is recorded that in the morning they were all dead bodies.2 Kings 19:35 How could this happen? The "how can this happen" in the world are honestly nothing for God.

Our prayers as we live in today's world

As we live our lives, problems and worries arise. That is life. Each time, should we strive to use our human strength to solve them? The world is full of incomprehensible things; there are all kinds of people and things around you that make your life difficult. Each time, should you use your wits to set up countermeasures or is reflection and self blame the better option?

That is not the answer. Trying hard to solve the problem on our own is our force of habit; it is our nature. Thinking that you can do all things by your power, thinking you did not try hard enough when things do not work out and blaming yourself for making mistakes is not the true meaning of the walk of faith. It may sound silly but we often try to limit God's power with our brains. If you lose hold of why God, who makes no mistakes, allowed this situation to happen, you will truly be lost in a blind spot.

Frankly speaking, you cannot do anything, let alone evangelize by your own strength. Evangelism is the work of God and God is the one who does it. If you cannot understand this principle, evangelism will be most difficult and burdensome thing in the entire world. The same goes for your life. God exists, whether we acknowledge it or not. He knows the situation you are in; He even knows the tactics and schemes you used that got you there to begin with. Prayer is laying yourself down before the God who created you and has the best scenario for you.

Let's take another look at Jacob

Unaware of the mystery of prayer, Jacob was very shrewd and cunning. God granted troublesome events to Jacob and because of them, Jacob was forced to pray. That is God's providence. The covenant given to Jacob was truly amazing. When God called Abraham, Isaac, and Jacob, He called them already having the covenant of world evangelization. However, Jacob did not catch on to God's plan and used his tricks. He played hide and seek his entire life. He wandered aimlessly countless times even while holding to the covenant God gave him and finally, after many ups and downs, did he realize the meaning of his calling.

Examine yourself to see if your life is not similar to Jacob's. Do not surreptitiously sidle up to God when it looks like there is no other way after you have been worrying on your own for a couple of days. Just bring it before Him from the onset. Do you think you can estimate God's power with your guesses and level? Break free right now from the foolishness that tries to fit the limitless God into the mold of your shallow knowledge and experience. God is not the last ray of hope as you grasp for straws. He is the one who is more than able to take your everything, your all. Stand before the name of Jesus Christ.

Then everyone, students, employees, and even pastors need to stand before God. The one who stands before God can gain the spiritual strength that God gives. You cannot raise or lower your self worth. Of course our essence of being children of God does not change, but being human we cannot live outside of the influence of our circumstances and environment so our cognitive process for interpreting external factors is very important. The promise to guard our hearts and our minds^{Philippians 4:6~7} becomes even more appealing from this standpoint. Starting now, moment by moment, see, hear, think, imagine, remember and decide in front of God.

David

Think about when you wake up in the morning. There are days when it is so difficult to get up and then there are days you feel relaxed and refreshed. There are days you wake up in a good mood and there are days you do not. The author of Psalm chapter 17 writes, "when I awake, I shall be satisfied with your likeness." Psalm 17:15 This was David's confession and prayer as a child of God. What does it mean to be satisfied with the Lord's likeness when you awake from your slumber?

Baring your soul in prayer

As you live your life, you may face frustrating situations or problems you simply cannot understand. You may even face unfair situations that leave you wondering, "Why did this happen to me?" as well as find yourself in situations that you make you feel helpless. At those times, unbelief and resentment may begin squirming inside your heart. If you cannot pray, you will not be able to handle the various problems and worries that arise in life. A child of God should be able to bring anything in prayer before God. If you have the mystery of prayer, then you have everything.

When you pray, you enjoy the spiritual facts. Each time you pray, the spirit of God, the Holy Spirit, works and the evil spirit, Satan, and the forces of darkness crumble. Therefore, prayer is the science and mystery for enjoying the spiritual facts that God has given. If you do not know prayer, then you are unaware of the vast majority of the walk of faith. However, if you know the mystery of prayer, no matter what kind of hardships come, you will be able to unravel them as well as realize God's hidden plan. Just pray about the worry you have right now before God. Look at David's confession.

• Psalm 17:1
Hear a just cause, O Lord; attend to my cry!
Give ear to my prayer from lips free of deceit!

When you honestly confess before God, God hears that prayer and answers. Have you ever worried because praying is difficult or you do not know what to say? Just pray this way, "God, I'm not sure how I should pray." Just as you are right now, bare your soul before God. Of course baring your soul does not mean whining, groaning, or complaining to God.

• Psalm 17:4~5
With regard to the works of man, by the word of your lips
I have avoided the ways of the violent.
My steps have held fast to your paths; my feet have not slipped.

David always followed God's Word. When God's people receive God's Word, they receive great grace and answer.

• Psalm 17:7
Wondrously show your steadfast love,
O Savior of those who seek refuge
from their adversaries at your right hand.

The right hand usually signifies strength. David did not merely say God's power; he expressed it as God's right hand. He was always experiencing God's powerful hand in his life.

• Psalm 17:8
Keep me as the apple of your eye; hide me in the shadow of your wings.

This confession is the answer to what happens when we pray. Every part of our body is important, but there is probably no organ more sensitive and important than the eye. God guards His children like the apple of His eye and promises to hide them in the shadow of His wings. How full of peace and grace are these words?

The reason their prayers and your prayers are different

Then how should you pray? Inscribe the following three things in your heart as you pray, and then answers will absolutely come.

First, enjoy the Gospel. What we, as those who have crossed over from death to life through Jesus Christ, must do is simply meditate on and confirm our God-given status as well as utilize our authority. Not our nature or thoughts but seeking God's grace and plan is the Gospel-centered prayer.

Second, enjoy the Gospel as you do your work, think, and make decisions. Our everyday thoughts are just as important as our prayers. Many things will differ depending on what thoughts we have. The reason is that the direction and content of our prayers are greatly connected to our past experiences, memories, thoughts, and emotions. It goes without saying that answers to prayer differ depending on the direction and content of our prayers. Our everyday thoughts come off in our prayers and those prayers manifest as answers in our lives. Completely empty the complicated thoughts, unbelief, grudges, and obstinance filling your brain right now.

Third, God grants amazing answers and evidence to those who have a mission for the Gospel and for the evangelism that reveals God's glory. If you are worried about problems in your workplace or business, receive grace through worship, and once you gain strength, live the life of the evangelist. Furthermore, enjoy the answer of being a family that evangelizes and does missions down through the generations.

This is a request to those about to enter school, the workforce, or those who are turning over a new leaf in life. Plan how you will enjoy the Gospel in prayer, how you will enjoy the Gospel through your thoughts, and how you will live a life for the sake of the Gospel. From that day on, you will be inspired by the grace God gives you every morning when you open your eyes and joy and peace will well up from the depths of your soul.

"When I awake, I shall be satisfied with your likeness."

Jesus' prayer

The world-renowned consultant Dale Carnegie wrote that 70% of all our worries are financial. There is some truth to that. Poverty makes people wretched. On top of that, if you have nowhere to turn for help, you become even more miserable and begin to look pathetic in your own eyes. To make matters worse, if you do not have any abilities, all you can do is sit around breathing out sigh after sigh.

However, Solomon, who possessed great wealth, confessed that those who long for money may obtain it but will never be satisfied. He means that money may help you get things but it cannot give you lasting satisfaction.

Before concluding His earthly ministry and right before bearing the cross, there was one final thing that Jesus did. He prayed. Seek out the important things as you look at Jesus' prayer.

Jesus who prayed in the face of crises

Jesus asked God about everything. That is pretty significant! If even Jesus prayed, then it goes without saying that we must stand before God.

As we live our lives, we may face misunderstandings that leave us dumb-founded. We can get swept up in unwanted conflicts that put us in an awkward position. What should you do in these kinds of situations? Have you tried standing before God? Do not perk up your ears to listen to the tidbits the people around you offer, swaying you this way and that way; just ask God. God will answer to your conscience. If you stand before God, He will give the definite answer to your heart and mind. Every time a worry rears its ugly head in your life, repeat this question to yourself, "What would Jesus do?"

Everyday prayer

Praying in the face of crises was not the only prayer Jesus taught us. Jesus did not desperately pray not knowing what else to do when the waves suddenly began to crash over Him. Jesus prayed in His everyday life; He arose early in the morning and went off to a solitary place to pray.

• Mark 1:35
And rising very early in the morning, while it was still dark,
he departed and went out to a desolate place, and there he prayed.

Jesus is the Son of God and the Christ who solved all of mankind's problems. Those who believe this fact can pray and experience the God who answers prayers. Do you know what prayer is? Prayer is the key that opens the doors of heaven; something that can never be done by our effort or our brains. It is the authority that can break down the forces of darkness that no power or wealth can stand against. Those who enjoy the mystery of prayer understand their past and present, and gain the wisdom to clearly see their future. They can sit still and move the world.

We must remember the following things from Jesus' prayer.

First, pray in front of God, not in front of people. God saved you with His overflowing love and He planned to do world evangelization through you. Therefore, if we sincerely pray before God, God will answer all our prayers and supply us with the very best things.

Next, get into the habit of praying in your everyday life. This was the example Jesus set and taught. Wake up in the morning and leisurely pray. As you lay down to sleep, examine your day and stand before God. Throughout the day, at the most important time, look to God. From that point on, God's grace and blessings will flow through your life. Aligning your entire day, that is, your schedule, meetings, and movements to God is true prayer.

If you are living like someone who has nothing even after you have received everything, the fault most definitely lies with you. The reason Jesus called us was to be with us and He promised to be with us to the very end of the age.

Do not be concerned
with how people look at you,
Simply lay down everything before God:
do not hold anything back.
Tell Him everything.

Let go of your own strength.

All that you have planned,
All the things you wanted to do,
All your thoughts and ways
Lay them all down.
Seek and find God's
will, plan, and ways.

Chapter 04

Prayer becomes fun when you receive answers

Let's be frank.
Do prayers really come true?

"Hm.. That's strange. It should be right there; can't you see it?"

These days, you rarely see a car that does not have a navigation system. However, in the past, people would find their way with hand-drawn maps. I remember times when I just could not figure out the map and had to make several phone calls before finally finding my way. Whenever that happened, it was really frustrating and upsetting to hear the person on the other end of the line say, "Hm, that's strange. It should be right there; can't you see it?"

To the person who knows the way, any road they take is easy. However, if you do not know the way, it is easy to get lost. Furthermore, if the map is drawn incorrectly, filled with scribbles and arrows, the frustration grows exponentially. And what about asking for directions in countries whose land mass is vast to begin with. In places like Russia or China, people say, "It's not far" when describing places that are 3 hours away by car. From their perspective a 3 hour drive is just around the corner.

Then what about your life road? Are you laboring along with an incorrect map? Do you lose your nerve and get swept up with the crowd over one word someone says to you? When you look at your life, do you feel the rush of racing down a wide-open highway or is it filled with the questions marks of your fears and doubts?

Looking at us, Jesus says:

• John 14:6
I am the way, and the truth, and the life.
No one comes to the Father except through me.

Is life wearing you down?

Mankind's suffering began with separation from God. However, most people do not even know the reason why they face failure, suffer, receive scars, and are hurting over the endless troubles that come their way. With no solution in sight, people live their lives like slaves, bound to something. They are captives

If you have a poor sense of direction
it is easy to get lost in a place you
have never been before.

Which way should you go?
You look around,
wondering if you will ever reach
your destination.

However, if you have a poor sense
of direction regarding your life path,
then that is a bigger problem.

If you know,
"Who you are," and "Where you are,"
then you will not be shaken
or alarmed no matter who says
what to you.

to, obsessed with, or addicted to money, gaining fame, their interpersonal relationships, games, shopping, drinking, dancing, studies, and the like. Otherwise, they would not be able to bear their unhappy lives.

Not knowing the Gospel means that you do not know who you truly are. Then it is rightful that you do not receive answers to prayer. Jesus Christ fulfilled the covenant that the offspring of woman would crush the head of the serpent and the Israelites were delivered from Egypt the day they put the lamb's blood on their door posts. The covenant of Immanuel given to the Israelites during captivity was fulfilled. Anyone who has gained happiness through the Gospel can relay the Gospel they know to the people who are still lost in darkness, chaos, and void. This is evangelism. Furthermore, God has prepared those appointed for salvation. We are not evangelizing to them through our eloquence but if we can evangelize them through our lives, then our lives are truly a success.

Not receiving answers to prayer is strange

Have you received salvation? Are you a child of God? The God who saved you from the miry quicksand will guard you all the days of your life. Jesus safeguards us in the name of the Father and wants us to be filled with joy. From the throne of heaven, Jesus blesses the church and considers each and every one of us as He prays. Jesus is the beginning and the end and with the two-edged sword He watches over you with eyes like flames of fire and feet like burnished bronze.

Are you discouraged because you lack the background that can provide fame and wealth? Remember that even though you live in this world, you do not belong to this world; you have been set apart. The creator God who called you is the source, the beginning. If you pray in the name of Jesus Christ, God will answer. The person who has their own time of prayer has the rhythm of their life in place. When you hold to the Word and pray, you will see God's time schedule regarding the field. At times, you may grow tired and weary. Even then, enter into deep prayer. Then what is "deep prayer?" Do not be concerned with how people look at you. Simply lay down everything before God; do not hold anything back. Tell Him everything. Let go of your strength. All that you were planning, all the things you wanted to do, all your thoughts and ways, lay them all down. Seek and find God's will, plan, and ways.

Simply think that you will be the person who prays the most in the entire world and connect everything you think about to prayer. Even when you make mistakes and when things happen that make you boil with rage, make the resolution to assuage it with prayer.

The lighthouse that protects the fishing boats on the night sea faithfully guards its post with its beacon every day of the year and for countless years to come. Just live your life like that lighthouse. One day, those lost in the darkness will, one by one, find their way to your beacon of the Gospel.

Do you know
the power of prayer?

• Jeremiah 33:2~3
Thus says the Lord who made the earth,
the Lord who formed it to establish it
– the Lord is his name: Call to me and I will answer you,
and will tell you great and hidden things that you have not known.

The son of a king can fully enjoy the power his father wields whenever and wherever. God is the king who created the world and mankind and He has sovereignty over our lives with power and unlimited wisdom beyond our thoughts or expectation. God has already placed authority in the hands of His children. However, there are many times when God's children forget their status and mope about, dejectedly holding their head in their hands in the face of life's important problems.

God called you having already prepared the best path for

your life. Therefore it is rightful that you face hardships when you try to break down a door God has intentionally closed or you try to break through a wall that is not even a door. Is there anything more safe or trustworthy than receiving God's guidance? If God opens the door, turn your eyes, make plans, and follow through in that direction. What if God does not open the door? Just wait until He does; there is nothing to worry about.

Then, what should you do now?

Everything depends on everyday prayer

Do you want to enjoy the answer Joseph received in Genesis chapter 39? Since the Lord was with Joseph, he steadfastly received God's answers whether he was a slave, in prison, and even when he became governor. Who can harm or topple the person God has chosen?

Starting today, even if it for just one minute, give yourself just as you are to God. When you try praying for 1 minute, you will see it can be both easy and difficult at the same time. It does not seem like much to take out 1 minute from the 1,440 minutes you have in a day. However, if your life is not aligned with God, then giving yourself wholly to God for 1 minute is impossible. The person who can give 1 minute of their 1,440 minutes to God will find that the rest of the 1,439 minutes is aligned with God. Then it is rightful that God would give that person the wisdom of heaven and overflowing health that the world cannot comprehend. Moment by moment, converse with God. When something special or important comes up, they are the golden opportunities to pray with all your heart, so do not lose hold of them!

If it is God's will, do not hesitate

If everyday prayer is established in your lifestyle and you sense that this is God's plan, go with it. When Moses realized God's will and extended his staff, the Red Sea parted. When the feet of the priests bearing the Ark of the Covenant stepped into the Jordan River, the waters receded. For God's children who pray, there are times when their interest and God's desire line up in this way. Do not stumble about stupefied by the events unfolding before you. Quickly catch on to what is really happening and realize that the time to taste God's power has finally come. God did not break down Jericho with a grand display of His power and then tell the Israelites to go in. God broke down the walls of Jericho when the Israelites took the steps and circled the city in faith.

Make a resolution

When Abraham resolved to offer his one and only son to God, God prepared the ram and showed him the mystery of salvation. In Genesis chapter 22, when Daniel staked his life and made a resolution, he received a great answer that surprised all the people of the world. Daniel's three friends did not pray, "We are facing a hardship, please save us." They resolved in their hearts to give their lives to follow God's will. God saw their hearts and guarded their lives. The living God is listening to your prayers even now. More accurately speaking, not only does God see our hearts and our thoughts, He knows what we lack, what we sincerely desire and what we need better than we do.

Life of a witness, really?

When God's child goes to the field, God works full-fledged. Then what kind of evidence must we have in the field? Not only did Christ take up all the problems of our lives but keep in mind that, moment by moment, He is with us everywhere we go. Never forget that He has a plan no matter who you meet or where you meet them.

Starting today, pray that the work of the Holy Spirit, which no one can block, will arise in the place where you are! Pray that the doors of evangelism, which God desires, will open, that the Word will be fulfilled, and that disciples will arise. This is the evidence God wants to give to you in the field. The person who can feel God's touch in the very place where they are is the one that knows the true joy of living.

They say that prayer can
move mountains

If you buy jewels or electronic equipment you receive a certificate of authenticity. This is a document that certifies that the product you bought is authentic. Have you received your certificate as God's child? Then, you need to receive God's guidance. The filling of the Holy Spirit is fully enjoying Immanuel, the fact that God is with you in your life.

Largely, there are three kinds of answers to prayer. The answer comes in the way you prayed, answers come differently from how you prayed, and there may not seem to be any answers. However, all three cases are answers and God's most fitting guidance for each situation. The person who prays can see the future that God prepares and plans.

God's child can see God's plan when he prays. Jesus too prayed without sleeping. The Reverend John Wesley said that prayer is the believer's main occupation.

Honestly speaking, we are reluctant to expose our shortcomings or flaws in front of others. There is not a single person who enjoys having his problems pointed out or criticized by others. However, there is no reason to deceive or hide anything in front of God. How reassuring is that. God knows everything and accepts everything with no ill will. As you look at your entire life, find the plan God desires and the way in which He is fulfilling that plan.

Then, all we have to do is pray?

• Psalm 5:3

O Lord, in the morning you hear my voice;
in the morning I prepare a sacrifice for you and watch.

Just pray in your best time, in the manner that is most fitting for your lifestyle. Setting aside a certain time to pray throughout your day will greatly enhance your life of following God's guidance. Of course, if you take time early in the morning to pray, you can listen to God's Word with a fresh mindset and it will help you concentrate in prayer better. Praying early in the morning and studying is a great way for students to improve in their studies.

Just think of your prayer time as the best time you set apart to gain strength.

Solving the problem with answer key in hand

There is no surer way to answers than finding your prayer topics while looking at God's plan. Have you ever racked your brains to solve a math problem, and then slapped your knee in realization as you looked at the answer key and saw how the problem was solved? It is the same when we pray with the prayers topics we uncover from God's plan. Honestly, we do not have the power, wisdom, or background to move mountains. However, the Holy Spirit works, the forces of darkness crumble, and Satan's schemes fall through when we pray. Not only that, God's angels carry out God's will.

If it is something anyone can do, then we do not need to pray. Does the future look bleak and are you backed up against your limitations without a clue as to what you should do? God has already given you the answer key. What are you waiting for? Open it up and take look.

You need a key to open the door of answers

What to do first

Jesus spoke about what must be done first. In Matthew 5:24, Jesus says to reconcile with your brother before you come to worship. More than saying that worship is unimportant, this verse means that we should take care of the anger and misunderstandings we have with others and be reconciled with them in order to give true worship.

More than rattling off the things I want one by one, it is better to "seek first the kingdom of God and his righteousness."^Matthew 6:33 Like the words of Matthew 7:1-5, we must see the log in our own eye first rather than the speck in our brother's eye and being able to do that will benefit us as well. A log, simply put, is like a pillar. How can you see the speck in your brother's eye when you are firmly clutching a pillar that blocks your line of sight? That is why, examining yourself comes first.

Jesus also speaks about forgiveness. There was a man who was in debt for 10,000 talents. It was such a large amount of money that it was difficult to even fathom. Even though he wanted to pay off the debt, there was no way he could. Knowing that he would be thrown in jail if he could not pay off the debt, his master took pity on him. So his master told the servant that he did not have to pay off the debt and his debt was cleared. How do you think the servant felt? I am sure he felt an inexpressible wave of joy and relief. On his way home, he ran into a person who owed him 100 denarii. It would have been so great if he had said,

"Hey, I feel so great today. I was so worried about my debt but it was all resolved today. You must have had a hard time too worrying about paying back the 100 denarii. You don't have to worry anymore. I clear you of your debt." However, he did not say this. He grabbed the man who owed him the money by the collar and shouted, "How wicked you are! How long has it been since you borrowed that money and you still haven't paid me back!"

What was the reason Jesus used this example? All the curses we should have received were cleared away by Jesus Christ's blood. Original sin and actual sins as well as all the curses and disasters that come from ancestral sins have all been resolved.

Then, do the mistakes and wrongdoing of our neighbors seem that great and unforgivable?

Three keys

God wants to answer His children. He has decreed to show great and hidden things that we have not known. God has set His heart to answer us but why are there no answers in our lives? Examine yourself to see if you have the following three keys.

The first is to look to God. How can we fathom God's plan when we do not even look to him 5 minutes out of the day. When we look to God, our bodies and minds become strong and refreshed. If those suffering from spiritual hardships would make time to look to God, they would absolutely get well.

Second, pray for financial blessings. This does not mean we should beg God to grant our wish to hit the lottery jackpot or become wealthy. However, for the person who believes in God to always be strapped for cash or wallowing in debt is strangely unbecoming and even pitiful. Giving offering for evangelism and missions and serving to build your church so that it can do the work of changing the region should not be a burden or be too much to expect. It should be rightful and joyous.

While I was a seminary student, I met a person who had a

passion for evangelism and was waiting to be commissioned to the missions field. I truly wanted to help him but I did not have even a penny to spare. That is why I prayed to God. The next week I went to school to pay my tuition and was told that someone had already paid my tuition for me. When I asked the secretary who had paid the tuition, she answered that she did not know and in addition, wondered why I did not know who it was.

I immediately sent the tuition money I had to the missionary. Even now, this is the prayer I never omit, the payer of blessing the precious church officers and believers who will work together with the evangelists. How can I not offer prayers of blessings upon those who will stand before God and serve through their finances so that the church can do world evangelization, the pastors can evangelize, and our posterity can realize their dreams to their hearts content.

The third key is the blessing of evangelism. Evangelism starts with enjoying the God who is with you. If God gives you evidence so that anyone who sees you can tell that you are a child of God, then you become His witness. Then when people see you and want to believe in God, evangelism naturally takes place.

Moment by moment, faithfully and concretely enjoy the complete Gospel that you have in your heart. The mystery to that lies within worship and prayer. In the time you spend face to face with God, God will absolutely work as you confirm the reason you must receive financial blessings and the reason you must live.

Are you ready?
Here come the answers

All religions have some form of "prayer." People think they can receive answers if they diligently pray and some even do. However, it is not God, but Satan who is giving those answers. So even though they got what they asked for, they will ultimately fail. We must receive the answer that God gives. Then there is something you must know to receive God's answers.

The pass code: Christ

• John 16:24
Until now you have asked nothing in my name.
Ask, and you will receive, that your joy may be full.

Christ is the most blessed gift God gave to us. It is the name of salvation promised to those lost in original sin, the name our forefathers of faith so longed and waited for, and the name that fulfilled salvation for mankind while they were separated from God, lost in sin, and enslaved by Satan. God answers everyone who has the name of Christ. Just like you need to know the pass code to open the door, the door of answers open when you have Christ.

The person who has Christ can seek out and enjoy the many blessings in Christ.Colossians 2:3 The blessing of the Holy Spirit being with you, guiding you and answering you, the blessing of the protection of angels, the blessing of breaking down the forces of darkness, the blessing of entering God's kingdom, and the blessing of living the life of an evangelist are all yours to enjoy.

A construction worker sent to Afghanistan by his company was taken hostage. What his family wants is not a luxury car or expensive clothes. They ask nothing more than that their kidnapped son return safely to their bosom as soon as possible. God's heart is the same. He wants His children to return to His bosom as soon as possible. That is why God absolutely answers the prayers of the evangelist who leads one soul back to Him.

If you know the pass code,
the locked doors

will open up before you.

Passwo

Four things

The following is what God's child must know and enjoy.

First. Everyday, newly enjoy the fact that Jesus is the Christ who completely solved all of mankind's problems. Most people become indifferent when exposed to the same thing over and over again. Then how different are you today from the day you were first moved by the gift of grace you received? Are you living your life as if you deserve all this, completely forgetting the time you spent in suffering and frustration? Think back on the time when you realized that Jesus Christ is the one who solved all the spiritual problems and worries that you could not resolve on your own. Enjoy the mystery of Christ more abundantly every day. Then you can truly live as a child of God. "Christ" is not the same name over and over again but the name that is new every day and that can lead you anew every day.

Second, experience the fact that Jesus Christ died according to scripture and rose again according to scripture. Jesus Christ did not simply die on the cross. He resurrected and is living and working even now. Not the Jesus that died on the cross for you a long time ago, but looking to the Jesus that is with you right now is the correct walk of faith. When you pray in the name of the resurrected Jesus, God works in you, with you, and in the places connected to you.

Third, experience the work of the Holy Spirit that appears in your life when you pray in Jesus' name. Acts chapter 2 records the fulfillment of the prophesied filling of the Holy Spirit from Joel 2:28. God took care of all your life problems and even now is living and working. When that God works through the Holy Spirit, evidence and answers appear in every facet of your life.

Fourth, Jesus Christ will return after the Gospel is proclaimed to all the world. Experience this promise. Matthew 24:14 states, "And this gospel of the kingdom will be proclaimed throughout the whole world as a testimony to al nations, and then the end will come." The reason the sun rises and sets, the reason the earth revolves is because there are people on this earth that need salvation. God wants all people to be saved and come to the knowledge of the truth. 1Timothy 2:4 The person who places God's desire in his heart will enjoy the blessing of finding the disciples whom God has prepared all over the place.

So do you have the pass code that opens the door of answered prayer? Then abundantly enjoy these four blessings in your life and truly see that the world is not worthy of you.

What exactly is answered prayer?

God is almighty. There is nothing God's power cannot do or cannot make happen. Then, when does God reveal His almighty power?

Do you see God's desire?

When I was young, an engineering student lived next door. His mother had him when she was young but because of all the hard work she had to do, her back was crooked and she was stooped over. She always walked around leaning on a cane. One day, her son passed out from gas inhalation. When she heard the news, she tossed aside her cane and started running. They rushed him to the hospital and thankfully, he recovered. The next day, she was hobbling around on her cane once again as if the previous day's event had never happened. How earnest must her heart of love for her son have been to give her that kind of strength? Then what makes your heart earnest?

When we know God's desire, God's plan, and follow it, we can experience the almighty power of God. Regardless of how much or how little we have, if we embrace God's desire and follow God's plan, God has no choice but to answer us. God works with His power upon the believer and the church that holds to His desire. When you realize, "Evangelism is God's desire. God wants all people to hear the Gospel and be saved," and match your direction to evangelism, you will see evidence and answers you never enjoyed before. Everyone has wondered at least once, "What am I living for? What must I live for?" If you decide you must study for the sake of evangelism, God will give you wisdom. If you decide you must run your business for the sake of evangelism, God will be with you in power.

The prayer topic that becomes more complete

There are many teenagers, college students, and adults who say with a worried face, "Praying is not that easy."

Prayer is a steady process that gradually reaches completion. When you know God's desire regarding souls and find your prayer topics within His far-reaching yet meticulous plan, then prayer will take place automatically.

As you pray, your prayer topics are revised and supplemented. That is how your prayer topics are brought to completion. You write down your prayer topics in your notebook, right? Take some time to look back on the lifelong prayer topic you wrote down at the beginning of the year, your prayer topic for this year, and your prayer topic for this month. As you see how your prayer topics were revised and supplemented, you will gain unexpected revelations.

The walk of faith is truly joyous!

The person who embraces God's desire and the prayer topics that are on their way to completion, finds their answers becoming more solidified through the Word they receive from the worship every week. Realizations come as you listen to the Word and you gain strength that you never felt anywhere else. You may not memorize the sermon word for word, but the grace you received from the Word will come to mind, moment by moment, throughout the week. Then when you go to the field with the Word you received, you will experience the Word being fulfilled. When you go to the field, answers will already be there but problems and incidents can also arise. However, never forget that God has hidden answers and blessings inside of incidents and problems. If you gain the wonderful and amazing strength that God gives, you will fully be able to overstep your circumstances and the deep-rooted problems you find there.

Now is the time to resolve in your heart

God can do all things. That is why God's child has no reason to fail. Then what is the reason God's children get lost in the thinking, "I'm a failure" and do not enjoy their blessings as a child of God in their life?

I never learned Japanese when I was young, but I remember using Japanese words quite frequently. My parents lived through the Japanese occupation so I picked up those words from hearing them use them. For 36 years, Japan occupied Korea and the Japanese culture infiltrated into even the Korean language.

Then what about the Israelites who were enslaved by Egypt for 400 years? Each time the Israelites served idols, powerful nations like Assyria, Babylon, and Philistine invaded and took Israel captive. They were colonized by Rome and ultimately the entire nation was scattered across the world. Not only Israel, but in each age, the other nations were no exception. Each time a nation became filled with idols and the culture of not believing in God spread throughout the land natural or man-made disasters and calamities crashed in.

It is the same today. Satan is infiltrating people through idols. Under Satan's control, people commit heinous crimes and wars are breaking out all over the world. What is even more serious is the fact that idolatry and the culture of not believing in God have nonchalantly settled in around us. There are countless booths and shops filled with psychics and tarot readers. Trying to justify itself under the lofty guise of respecting individuality, pluralism states that it is all right as long as you sincerely believe in something. And people adhere to it as the most rational line of thinking.

What must you do in this kind of world to enjoy answers worthy of a child of God? In each age, the people used by God took a stand against the forces of idolatry and saved their nation. If you simply resolve in your heart to give your life for this, God will give you evidence.

God saved the Israelites through Daniel who read God's heart. Although he was taken as a captive, Daniel so distinguished himself that his superiors noticed him and even became an official trusted by the king. At that time, some jealous officials found out that Daniel prayed for his nation three times a day to God and used that to conspire against him. They proposed to the king that anyone who prays to anyone else but the king for the next 30 days should be cast into the den of lions. The king signed the document with his seal. Knowing that the document had been signed, three times a day, Daniel opened his windows towards Jerusalem and prayed giving thanks to God just as he had done before. When Daniel was arrested, the king was quite distressed for he favored Daniel but he had no choice, it was the law. The night Daniel was cast into the den of lions, the king spent the night fasting, with no diversions and no sleep. Then at the break of day, the king arose and hastened to the den of lions.

• Daniel 6:20
O Daniel, servant of the living God,
has your God, whom you serve continually,
been able to deliver you from the lions?"

Then from within the den, Daniel greeted the king as he always greeted him. God saved Daniel from the den of lions. Just as no one was able to block God's power when He worked upon Daniel, if your life is in God's hands, then no one can block you. Isn't that so?

A prayer of resolution

First is the prayer of holding to the covenant. Separated from God, we lived suffering from the forces of sin, Satan, and curses but Jesus Christ delivered us and now we enjoy freedom. Anyone who does not meet God will fail. However, even if you are a child of God, if you do not receive answers to prayer, you will suffer in life. When you pray the prayer of enjoying this mystery of the Gospel, you receive answers.

Second, set your heart on what God desires. Daniel believed that God was alive, and after setting his heart on fighting against the idols, he resolved not to defile himself with the food offered to idols. When Daniel set his heart and resolved, God granted him the grace of looking better and fatter in the flesh than all the youths who ate the king's food. As you meditate on the Word God gives you, you can make the resolution that befits your situation and position. That is the very place where answers begin.

Third, enjoy answers every day through prayer. Daniel knew that the king signed the document but he still went to his home, opened his windows towards Jerusalem, and prayed. Making God's will regarding the Israelites the desire of his heart, he got on his knees and earnestly prayed. When we designate a time and pray for world evangelization, God works. Through the people who prayed knowing the spiritual mystery, God raised the works of life in each age. As Daniel stepped out of the den of lions, he confessed, "My God sent his angel and shut the lions' mouths, and they have not harmed me." God works the moment we begin praying.

Lastly, enjoy everyday prayer to the point that God's will becomes your life's motto. If there is anyone who resolves in his heart, "God wants to rescue this age from idolatry. It would be great if God uses me for this," then God's works will appear through that person.

Continuous prayer means the state where the frequency of our thoughts, emotions, and actions are always in tune with God. It is at this time, God gives us the wisdom to see the future and opens our eyes to see history and this age. Make the resolution to be the evangelist who kneels in prayer for this age just like Daniel prayed for his nation. Match your life direction to God's will in calling you as an evangelist to reform the idolatrous culture of this age.

• Daniel 6:10
When Daniel knew that the document had been signed,
he went to his house where he had windows
in his upper chamber open toward Jerusalem.
He got down on his knees three times a day
and prayed and gave thanks before his God,
as he had done previously.

Have you found it yet?

You may be breezing through life, when all of a sudden, or more often than you like, something happens that makes your emotions erupt and leaves you feeling upset and uneasy. These incidents may stem from your mistakes or because of another's misunderstanding or mistake. Something so trivial can blow out of proportion and disrupt the entire situation. There will be some people who take it all in stride saying, "That's life," and there will be others nervously jumping about not knowing what to do. Instead of wallowing in regret and guilt or spewing out resentment and complaints at others, take a step back and reflect on that situation.

When answers do not come to your somewhat legitimate prayers it is not only rightful but something you should be thankful for. There are many people who bemoan the fact that they do not have answers to prayer. However it is most likely because they do not have the correct prayer topics. God is not some terrible God who stands by and watches His children as they frustratingly beat their chests and throw tantrums amidst their distress. The reason there are no answers is simply that we did not pray correctly or prayed for something ridiculous.

Then how can we hold to the correct prayer topics and become deeply entrenched in the life of answered prayers?

The habit of prayer, the prayer nature

The most important thing is for prayer to permeate throughout your life. I used the word "prayer nature" in hopes that it will help you more easily understand this kind of life habit or lifestyle. No matter what happens or if nothing happens, whatever you do or do not do, wherever you go or if you do not go anywhere and just sit there, if you can pray in all circumstances then prayer has truly become a part of your nature. If you have a prayer nature, that is, if you can change all your time to prayer, then you life will absolutely triumph.

They say that the habits you learn at three will last until you are eighty, but getting into the habit of praying will not happen overnight. There may be exceptions but the longer you lived according your own views and stubbornness, the harder it will be change all that. The person who first learns prayer as climbing up to a mountain and staying there all night, will think that is prayer. Those who saw people cry out to God until their voices become hoarse will think that is prayer. That is why the very first prayer you learn is so important.

This is prayer

The prayer you pray when you are alone comes first. Just as David praised and wrote confessions of faith while he was alone in the fields, get up in the morning, read the bible and meditate on the Words. As you meditate, take the things that hit your heart and confess your faith to God while earnestly seeking God; this is prayer.

Looking at the field you go to everyday with spiritual eyes is also prayer. If this habit pervades in your life, you will sensitively feel how God is with you in the field, then you will seek His guidance and assistance. Furthermore, you will see the people suffering spiritually because they have not met God. Your heart will also mourn for those who have become God's children but have become discouraged and live powerless lives.

If you are enjoying the mystery of prayer to this extent, then you will not need to ask, "What should I pray for?" This is because you know how people are struggling in various forms amidst suffering. You also know how great and gracious is the salvation you have received. You can see the countless people in this world living in unhappiness never having heard the news of salvation.

Now, what else must we pray for? There is nothing more important than deeply and abundantly enjoying the blessing of salvation you have received. Pray that the Jesus Christ, who solved all of life's problems, will be the Christ in your life and your master. Then God's kingdom will come not only on yourself, but also on every place where you are, on all the people you meet and you will stand as the witness that all must acknowledge.

Now that you know the reason God answers the one who has a prayer nature, and what is the prayer topic that God wants, start praying today. Pray that the Holy Spirit, the spirit of Jesus Christ, will rule over your thoughts, the ones you are aware of and even the ones that are in the recesses of your unconscious. Ask Him to work upon your complicated emotions and in every corner of your life. Then the dark thoughts and shadows stemming from the unbelief inside of you will completely disperse before the name of Jesus Christ and you will enjoy the happiness of having only the glorious light of Christ shine through your life.

If you do not have any answers
it is either one of two things.
You either lack faith or lack desire.

No matter what happens
or if nothing happens,
whatever you do or do not do,
wherever you go
or if you do not go anywhere
and just sit there,
if you can pray in all circumstances
then prayer has truly become
a part of your nature.

Chapter 05

So now what must you do?

You must know yourself
in order to pray correctly

Logically speaking, worrying about things that you have no control over is useless. This is because no matter how much you worry about it, you cannot change or control anything by your own strength. Worrying about things that have already happened is equally as foolish. Nothing good can come out of constantly thinking negative thoughts regarding things that have yet to happen or things that have already come to pass. We know all of this, but the problem lies with the regret and anxiety that inevitably seeps into us.

Several times a day, we find ourselves tragic heroes of misfortune or even the happiest people in the world. At times, we live our lives devoid of all emotion, and at other times, we fight countless wars against the "other you" hidden deep within. Because of uncontrollable emotions, we bother those around us and inflict wounds upon ourselves. We ultimately fall into despair and begin to resent God.

Many people realistically place greater importance upon their own thoughts and feelings rather than the working of the Holy Spirit. The fact that your thoughts and emotions are taking precedence simply means that you do not correctly know about the working of the Holy Spirit. Those who do not know about the working of the Holy Spirit, in turn, do not believe in the Word of God. If we do not believe in the Word of God, we are akin to unbelievers. We must find ourselves. When this happens, our hearts and bodies will be healed and everything will become more comfortable. If we cannot find ourselves in the Gospel and search for other things instead, everything will become more difficult. The mistakes of our past are not problems. There is no need for us to worry about the emotions that consume us moment by moment.

Then, what must we do?

Just because we run away in order to avoid the problem does not mean that the problem is resolved. Rather, "because" of those troublesome problems, we must discover the answer that God has given. Pray until you find your true self. This is the mystery to gaining inner strength within the grace of God.

If the problems that have accumulated from our childhood are not addressed, unbeknownst to us, those problems will become "scars," leading us to react sensitively to particular situations. The older we get, the more obstinate we will become, and on top of that, we will become all the more inflexible in our ways, causing the people around us to get increasingly frustrated. If we contract a physical illness, our lives will become even more unbearable. In addition, if we do not gain spiritual strength, our scars will only fester all the more. When we look at our environment and the problems that surround us, we will only fall into greater discouragement. When this turns into a vicious cycle, we will grow all the more exhausted. In this weak state, we absolutely cannot overcome the world. We must first acknowledge that we need God's grace more than anyone else. Take your current state and your present situation and go before God. You can continue this search for your true self all-lifelong. Actually, it is good for you to ask this question before God and receive the answer to your question.

If you are earnest,
your mindset becomes different

When you do college ministry, it is not easy to find students who are satisfied with their school or their field of study. Rather than determining their career path in light of their talents and interests, most students determine their future depending on their grades or follow the path that their parents have set for them. As a result, they cannot adjust to college life, and even if they go to study overseas, many of them resort to wandering aimlessly.

According to the Statistics Korea Bureau's "Social Statistics Research Findings," the percentage of students who are satisfied with their major, including the 13.0% that are "extremely satisfied" are 44.4%. This shows that the remaining 55.6% of students are not satisfied. Among them, 10.4% of students are "dissatisfied" and most of these students give up in the middle of their studies to either change their major or study an additional year to enroll in a different college.

Of course, there are also students who have plenty of ability and skill but are hard-pressed because they do not have the supportive background that is conducive to receiving a good education. We must help the next generation correctly recognize their skills and aptitude, as well as their interests, in order to take hold of clear goals and rise to the challenge to pursue their vision. This is the movement that is truly needed to save our posterity.

Luke 18:8 reads, "I tell you, he will give justice to them speedily. Nevertheless, when the Son of Man comes, will he find faith on the earth?" God is looking for none other than "faith." There are a few essential contents in the Bible. The promise that God will be with us is one such content. If it is surely the will of God, we must rise to the challenge, even though it may appear to be overwhelming or too difficult for us to handle. Even the unjust judge granted the widow justice. How much more so then, would God, who is our father, hear our prayers?

However, there is an important mystery contained within this parable. The widow did not ask for justice from the city mayor. She went in search of the one person who would be able to grant her justice. Likewise, who is the one we must pour out our petition to? We are praying to God who knows all things and can do all things. How can you expect that you will not receive answers when you are praying to such a God? That is why it is emphasized that what God looks at is our faith.

Also, what the widow was asking for was not something that was "great if it happened" and "too bad if it did not" depending on the circumstance. She had to receive justice. What is your all-consuming desire?

Finding it believable

There is a prayer of clinging to God, calling out to Him until you receive the answer. Perhaps this is the very start of prayer. Just as a hungry man goes to his friend to ask for some bread, just like a child throws a tantrum before his parents for something to eat. Because God has promised the Holy Spirit, if you refer to that promise and ask this of God, the answer will absolutely come.Luke 11:5~13

If you do not have a reason to pray, then you will find it difficult to receive answers. If you do not have answers, it is either one of two things. Either you lack faith, or you lack the desire.

When Daniel set his mind to pray special prayer, God sent the archangel to answer him.Daniel 10:10~20 In a single night, the Assyrian soldiers who were shouting murderous threats were wiped out. 2 Kings 19:35 This is the work that God carried out through His angels. Try setting a time to pray, praying moment-by-moment, and praying before giving worship.

You found yourself starting to pray

Though there is a stage in which you consciously try to pray, there is also a stage when you find prayer taking place without you even putting your mind to it. Joseph was like that in Genesis chapter 39, and Moses was like that in Exodus chapter 3. God changes and saves the age through people like this. The fact that prayer takes place means that you are unconsciously praying in your very life—within every and all situations, meetings, and even problems. These people are not shaken, even in the face of their personal limitations, frustrating circumstances, or problematic situations that seem to have no end. Just as Paul confessed in 1 Thessalonians 5:17 and Ephesians 6:18, if we enjoy prayer naturally in our lives, the eyes with which we interpret all events and the way that we react to the situations that arise will become all the more mature.

The admirable realm of transcending all things

How did Joseph, who was sold as a slave, rise to the position of governor? How did David, who was just a lowly shepherd, become the king of an entire nation? We are people who have realized the Gospel. When we pray, we will gain the strength to transcend ourselves. Our lives will change. We will overcome problems, surpass the age, and experience success in all manners. This is because we will come to possess the uniqueness that God gives.

May you perceive all things through the eyes of the Gospel. Confirm what your all-consuming desire is that is hidden deep within the recesses of your heart. Pray to God that He would reveal to you a greater and bigger plan, and when He does, don't hesitate; rise to the challenge.

What is the extent
of the power of prayer?

There are believers who worry about how they need to devote themselves. If you have a heart for evangelism and missions, you can place a region or a nation in your heart and set a prayer topic. Though it would be best for you to go directly, even if you do not go, you can still do missions. Praying sincere and heartfelt prayer is missions. If you pray for your family line to commission even one missionary and receive enough evidence to support that family, God will be pleased to answer you.

Healthy life

In order to devote yourself, health is of utmost importance. This is the very reason why God has given us our health. Though God can have a plan within sickness, the illness itself is not the will of God. God's will is for His children to be healthy and to triumph in all situations.

People can contract a disease through overexertion or by mistake, or even through an infection or simple old age. Besides these factors, there is a source of illness that the Bible reveals. Diseases came to be as a result of sin. Because of the original sin of being separated from God, as well as the unbelief that is passed down through the generations as a result of ancestral sin, the world continues to fall into illness. Households that worship idols from generation to generation have many spiritual problems and illnesses. Though this isn't applicable to all illnesses, there are also illnesses that are brought about by evil spirits. However, as 1 Corinthians chapter 12 reveals, there are also some illnesses through which God fulfills His will. For this reason, it is not wise to pass quick judgment on the nature of illnesses.

Needless to say, hospital diagnoses and prescription of medication is very useful. However, since there are some illnesses that come as a result of original sin and spiritual problems, we cannot rely solely on the physical. As we receive the help of specialized physicians and pharmacists, we must also keep in mind the order of healing. We must first gain spiritual strength. If we have fallen into hatred, anger, discord, or idol worship, the diseases of our hearts will not heal so easily. If at all possible, we must even change our environment. After that, we can proceed to receive physical therapy or treatment. As we receive healing, our faith is also an important factor. When we meditate on the fact that we have become children of God, as well as the grace and blessings we have received until now, a confession of thanksgiving will overflow from our hearts. When we have a thankful heart, the words of resentment and complaints, as well as the heavy burdens of our heart, will quickly dissipate, and we will be free.

Is the power of prayer that great?

When you pray in the name of Jesus during your prayer time, answers to prayer will come or works will arise. If you have an illness, proclaim in the name of Jesus Christ for that illness to depart from you. Command the spiritual problems flowing down your family line and the forces of failure to leave you. The works will arise. This is because the name of Jesus has power. When we restore our health through the name of Jesus, we will be able to overcome all of the hardships that have come to us individually and to our family lines.

Starting today, continue to have three discoveries. Whenever you give worship, whenever you work, and whenever you have meetings with other people, there is one thing that you must discover. It is invisible to the eyes, but you must be able to see the works of God. You must focus on the area in which God works. Experience the Word striking your heart and being brought to fulfillment and directly or indirectly experience the evangelism movement arising.

Enjoy these three things in your life and connect it with prayer. Then, connect your time of prayer with the worship on the Lord's Day. Surely, you will be able to see the amazing and great works of God that will leave you in astonishment. With this, you will be able to overcome the illnesses in your body, as well as the bitter roots within you that you are not aware of, the deep scars that you have, and the spiritual mannerism that repeatedly surfaces. If you are a child of God, you already have every right to experience the power of prayer.

You write a bucket list, but what about your lifelong prayer topic?

Newspapers, domestic and international alike, continue to report on the economic crisis and the recession. Most people, it seems, have a sense of the economic slump because of the situation of their own pockets. However, if you stop to think about it, there has never been a time when things weren't hard. Especially, with each passing day, the spiritual state of the world and the people of the world seems to grow increasingly poor, coarse, and dry. The emergency light has long since gone off in the field of politics and economics, and on top of that, people continue to face spiritual crisis and difficulty. Things only worsen and suffering continues because people do not have the basics of the Gospel and there is a lack of bright ideas to address these issues. Even believers are wandering, believing that evangelism is best left for special people.

For a time, writing a bucket list gained great popularity. Perhaps you have written one yourself. A bucket list is a list of things to do before you die. People often write their bucket list in a small notebook and feel a sense of accomplishment as they check off the things that they completed. Let us take a moment to ask a question. We take time to compile a bucket list of things to do; do we take that same amount of time to write our lifelong prayer topics?

As you record your lifelong prayer topics, you will come to know God's earnest desire for this age, the region, field, church, and even yourself. You will come to see what you must do. The answers that you will come to receive will become crystal clear.

Perhaps nothing is working out for you. Is your heart filled with complaints and resentment? Are you in the midst of hardship? It's all right! If you are living your life, completely oblivious of God's heart, and things go well with you, that is the greater problem. God knows that you have no background or knowledge. He knows that you are lacking in so many regards. He knows your powerlessness. That is why He is promised to give you strength and wisdom.

Your lifelong prayer topic is even more beneficial than a bucket list. How will you determine your prayer topics?

Buy the land where the hidden treasure is located

Setting our lifelong prayer topic is not so much a process of finding things to pray about but rather the discovery of what God wants to do through us through our lifetime as well as God's ardent desire. God didn't call Moses when he was young and able; He called Moses who was exhausted of all strength and 80 years old. God told Ananias that He had chosen Paul, the persecutor, as a vessel to fulfill God's desire among the Gentiles. God's plan and providence transcend our logic and level of knowledge. Oftentimes, His plan is far more dramatic and inspirational than any drama.

When the church and church officers do not receive answers, they have no choice but to place their interests elsewhere. The fact that the church does not have the influence or the strength to save the world is the saddest reality of all!

Do you know what God's desire is? It is for us to enjoy the Holy Spirit being with us, utilize the authority He has bestowed upon us, and experience the strength of that authority. It is for us to get a taste of the blessing of evangelism through which others realize that God is alive by looking at us. When we pray, the Holy Spirit works, unseen to our eyes, and the armies of angels fulfill the will of God. Can you see the field with the hidden treasure?

The way to begin all things

"O for a thousand tongues to sing my great Redeemer's praise, the glories of my God and King, the triumphs of His grace."

The Father of Methodism, John Wesley, penned the lyrics to this praise.

Whatever you do, the motive behind it all must begin from the blessing of salvation. Only then will you be filled with a spiritual life force and vigor. Only then will you have the content to relay to others through the blessings you have received. This is because you begin to have the leisure where you are able to share your blessings and give to others without regret.

God desires to save the world that has fallen into idolatry. However, if it is not by the power of creation, we cannot defeat the forces of darkness that are behind the idolatry. God is alive and is working even now by His Holy Spirit. He will grant power to those who seek it.

God works through those who know His desire. What we need the most right now is not a mouth that ceaselessly asks God to fill our requests, but the ears to hear God's voice and the eyes to perceive God's will.

Do you know continuous prayer?

"God, I don't have any money. That is why I will not rely on material wealth. I don't have a good educational background. That is why I won't rely on my own knowledge. I have no background or safety net to fall back on. God, please become my background. Send me to a church that will preach the Gospel."

20 years ago, this is the prayer that I prayed to God every morning.

Since then, I was able to preach the Gospel to my heart's content in my pastoral ministry. Even now, God continues to open the door of evangelism. Even now, I am experiencing the answer of the Gospel being testified throughout the world and disciples being raised. God absolutely answers the prayer given in faith.

As we live our lives, we are plagued by a vast array of worries.

Several times in each given day, we need to make important choices. We also need to make decisions regarding the important and minor problems and issues that arise in our lives. If we could only pray 24 hours a day, we would be able to make the choices that God desires. If we are led by God, great works will arise, but it is not so easy for us to pray without ceasing as we live our lives.

Answers do not discriminate between people

In Ephesians 6:18, Paul says, "Praying at all times in the Spirit, with all prayer and supplication. To that end keep alert with all perseverance, making supplication for all the saints." 1 Thessalonians 5:16~18 says, "Rejoice always, pray without ceasing, give thanks in all circumstances; for this is the will of God in Christ Jesus for you." In verse 25, it says, "Brothers, pray for us."

How did the prophet Elisha pray in the Old Testament? 2 Kings 6:8~23 reveals the answers that Elisha received. Elisha had such spiritual power that he even knew the plans of the king of Aram and reported this to the king of Israel. That is why Israel was able to foil all of the Aramean army's plans: when they attacked from the west, they would be prepared in the west; when they attacked from the east, they were ready for the offensive there, too. This was reported to the king of Aram, and the king issued the command to capture Elisha. As a result, countless Aramean soldiers surrounded the city of Dothan where Elisha was living. The servant who saw this grew fearful, but Elisha told him, "Don't be afraid for those who are with us are more than those who are with them." In 2 Kings 6:16, Elisha, who was always in prayer, was able to see the heavenly armies that were more powerful than the Aramean armies.

In this way, Paul and Elisha gained the strength of God through continuous prayer. Through prayer, we must restore our spiritual strength. If God answers us, we can receive answers. Then how can we receive answers?

There is something you must confirm

First, discard your unbelief and worries and pray. Then, you will receive answers. If you pray for God's will to be fulfilled rather than for your thoughts or plans to come to fruition, you will experience the works of God. When you pray knowing the spiritual facts, the heavenly armies will be mobilized and the door of evangelism will open. We are living in a complicated and dizzying world; for this reason, worries continue to plow into our thoughts. At this time, continuous prayer will become the driving force of our lives.

Second, whenever we pray, the Holy Spirit will work and the power of Satan will be broken. At that time, the problems that we have will begin to be resolved.

• Matthew 12:28
But if it is by the Spirit of God that I cast out demons,
then the kingdom of God has come upon you.

When the Holy Spirit works, the forces of Satan will crumble. At this time, the financial problems, interpersonal conflicts, and many other problems that have come as a result of sin and curses will begin to be resolved.

Third, when the angels that fulfill the will of God run their errands, we will receive answers to our prayers. You may ask whether angels truly exist or not. Let's look at the Bible for the answer.

• Hebrews 1:14
Are they [angels] not all ministering spirits
sent out to serve for the sake of those who are to inherit salvation?

• 2 Kings 19:35
And that night the angel of the Lord went out

and struck down 185,000 in the camp of the Assyrians.
And when the people arose early
in the morning—these were all the dead bodies.

When Peter was confined in the prison in Acts 12:1~10, God sent the angel to free Peter. Revelations 8:3~5 says that whenever we pray, God sends His angels to open the door of answers. In this way, God sends His angels for His children and fulfills His will. If we know this fact, we have every reason to pray.

But still

Because we have hit against hard times, perhaps it is difficult to make the choice of faith; or perhaps it seems easier to make decisions based on our own thoughts. However, there is one thing that we must remember. Prayer has a strength that far surpasses what we think; indeed, it exceeds our wildest imagination. We can break down the system of Satan that has filled the region in which we live through prayer. Through prayer, we can bind the evil spirits that gain a foothold over our thoughts.

What must we do when words of complaints and resentment flow from our mouth and we grow indolent from a lack of spiritual strength? Some people say that when we empty our hearts and discard our greed, we will be able to free ourselves from complaints. However, children of God can only lead happy lives when we are filled by the Holy Spirit.

Let's begin this prayer today.

"Send to me the armies that you sent to Elisha. Send me the angel you sent to Elijah and give me bread and water. Send the angel you sent to Hezekiah and get rid of the forces of darkness that hinder the proclamation of the Gospel. Send the angel you sent to Peter who was confined in prison and open all the blocked doors before me."

They learn
from watching you

The adults in the church may have heavy burdens and troubles weighing down their hearts. It is not easy to make a living in this competitive world and there are many things that need to be done inside the church as well. You need to correctly help your children and the church members as well as be a support to your pastor. You also have to prepare for your future and later years.

Show them what prayer is

Among the people in the Bible, Priscilla and Aquila were successful businesspeople. They knew about the work of the Holy Spirit. Do you believe that the Holy Spirit is with you and your children? If you are a child of God, you can experience the presence of the Holy Spirit. Experiencing the presence of the Holy Spirit means to enjoy the blessing of God being with you and this is the essence of prayer.

Remember Abraham. God promised to be with him and that no one would be able to overcome him. However, hardships continued to follow Abraham because there was unbelief hidden within him. In Genesis 13:14, "After Lot had separated from him." This was an important juncture. Accurately speaking, it means, "After Abraham made the decision of faith." This is the most fundamental and essential mystery: realistically enjoying the blessing of Immanuel in your life. God's children are the temple and the Holy Spirit dwells within them.1 Corinthians 3:16 When Jesus becomes the master of your life, a miracle arises.John 2:1-11 Therefore, if you receive the filling of the Holy Spirit, you will fully be able to save the world.Acts 1:8

You have to make many choices in life. At times, problems may arise. The resolutions of faith you make during these times are so important. Sometimes, making resolutions of faith may seem trivial. Resolutions are not only needed before great incidents, you need to make resolutions moment by moment in your everyday life. It can be difficult to make decisions of faith if you are only looking at your present reality. Honestly speaking, we are constantly making mistakes and stumbling through life because we lack strength and have shortcomings.

You find yourself thinking, wondering, and wanting to see.

Just because you like that person.

God's children must receive the guidance of the Holy Spirit in order to be happy. God promised that the Holy Spirit would be with us forever. That is why we must receive God's guidance. As Paul struggled to receive the guidance of the Holy Spirit, through him, the Gospel was spread throughout Asia[Acts 13] and the door of evangelism opened to Macedonia.[Acts 16] We live confronting the people of the world every day, that is why we must have the mystery of receiving the guidance of the Holy Spirit. When we do, God will absolutely raise us to the seat of success.

Gain the strength to save the world. The way to do that is to receive the filling of the Holy Spirit. The believers, who gathered in Mark's home to devote themselves to prayer, received the filling of the Holy Spirit and a miracle arose to overturn the entire world. The work of the Holy Spirit appeared, the prophesied Word was fulfilled, the doors of evangelism opened, disciples arose, and the field was changed. Then are all these works exclusive to only the Early Church?

What a good model of prayer!

I shared a conversation with a missionary receiving evangelism training. He was ministering in an impoverished and difficult region but someone sent him the message CD every week without fail. He spoke of how much grace and strength he received from the Word and he did not even know who that person was. Asking around, he found out that it was a young man in the church. It may seem like a simple task but it is not that easy to send the message and materials every week without fail for several years. This small deed saved a life and saved the field. You never know what kind of fragrant fruit will be borne from the small resolutions and actions you make today. Seeds sown in faith will absolutely be reaped in faith, in the most appropriate time and season.

The word "mystery" indicates something that is hidden or unknown. Anyone can pray but not everyone enjoys this blessing; that is why prayer is a mystery. In Romans 16:3-4, this one couple even risked their lives for Rome evangelization. If you look at the commentaries, they earned a great deal of money selling tents to Jewish people and Romans. Then let us take a look at God's heart that was compelled to bless these two, the businesspeople Priscilla and Aquila. Is there a more worthwhile life than Priscilla and Aquila's? They experienced the Holy Spirit, met the historic evangelist who would overturn the age and gave their entire life to God.

How will you find your balance between your social life,

church life, and family life? As mentioned before, experience the presence, guidance, and work of the Holy Spirit. If you have this strength, you will play the role of a missionary even though you are just a layperson. The children and youth in your church will one day become adults and raise other disciples. Your today of dreaming big dreams and faithfully doing the little things today will change your future.

You find yourself looking because it is so good

How do you walk? Do you need to tell your left leg to move in order for it to do so? You naturally walk without thinking about it. Do you know the famous golfer Ben Hogan? He started golf at the age of 12 and became a professional golfer by the age of 25. He won several tournaments and wrote an autobiography when he was 50. How much did he have to practice? When he hits the golf ball, does he think about what degree he should bend at the waist? Through countless hours of practice, he swings his club naturally with the form that has completely become a part of his body.

Countless thoughts cross our minds in our 24 hours. There are thoughts we are aware of but most of them we are unaware of. These thoughts stack up and become our nature. These thoughts and nature unwittingly become our lifestyle and our life.

God gave everything to His children. However, because of the nature that was hardened while we were separated from God and caught under the forces of darkness, we lose hold of the blessing of the Gospel. Then when we face a problem, we react according to our nature and resent God and do not believe in His power. After time passes, we realize that the problem was blessing but we fall into the same pattern again when we face another problem. If you stay in one position for a long time, you body becomes stiff since your blood does not circulate and you can even lose feeling. Is you life being restricted by your hardened thoughts?

Once again, everyday prayer is important

What is the most important thing for God's child? It is enjoying the blessing of the Gospel every day.

The Israelites were slaves in Egypt for a long time. At first, being a slave was hard but after several generations they became accustomed to being slaves, only vaguely awaiting the Messiah who would save them. God delivered the Israelites from slavery. However, the Israelites could not escape from the old nature of worshipping idols in Egypt and every time their bare necessities were not met they complained that they were better off as slaves.

As the Israelites were walking through the wilderness, God

made them construct the tabernacle and the altar for the burnt offering. Why did God tell the Israelites to build the tabernacle and the altar when they were busy enough just trying to get to Canaan? It was because they would not be able to conquer Canaan, the land to which the Messiah would come, with their slave nature. He wanted them to not be deceived by their hardened thoughts and to remember the Christ who would come to save them as they gazed upon the altar.

God had them make the tabernacle and live every aspect of their lives centered on the tabernacle. Why did He do that? The Israelites may have come out of Egypt but they continued to think like slaves. That is why God planned to make them enjoy Jesus Christ in their every day lives so that they would be able to escape from their nature of unbelief.

God wants the blessing of Jesus Christ to permeate throughout our lives. Are you still filling your life with other thoughts because you have lost hold of the joy in the Gospel even though you have received the Gospel? Change your nature with the prayer that enjoys the Gospel. Confess so that the savior Jesus Christ will become your Christ and the master of your life. If the time you spend focusing on the savior Jesus Christ is truly joyous, you will be able to overcome your wearisome environment and circumstances and even your wretched slave nature.

The blessings we have received are too great to waste our lives living with a nature of unbelief. A small resolution can bring about great change. Before you life becomes more set in the slave nature, make the time you spend focusing on God your most important time. Soon, you will not longer be trying to pray but just like swinging the golf club without thinking about it, you will find your soul, mind, life and sight fixed on God.

We often use say that prayer must take place. This means that prayer naturally and automatically runs its course in our lives. Do not call to mind the images of trying your best to pray. For lack of better expressions, casually looking to God, wanting to pray, constantly thinking of topics to pray about, prayer flowing from your lips, seem to be the closest way to describe prayer taking place in our lives.

If prayer takes place, then nothing can hinder it and nothing can be a problem. The time spent in prayer will be the most joyous time on earth. Without you even realizing, you find yourself just praying because praying just feels good. All other reasons disappear.

Pray for your marriage

There are times when diligently living your church life will not solve the problems you are facing. Jesus Christ solved all the problems on the cross, but you often wonder why life is so hard, and never-ending difficulties continue to follow you around.

The answer lies within the family

Often times the problems and difficulties that unceasingly knock on the door of our hearts come from our families. That is why it is important to find God's plan for you within the family. This means that whether you come from the picture perfect model of a harmonious home or from a family riddled with discord is not all that important. Most people do not turn their ears to the voice of God that can be heard in the family. They have settled into their family life without much fuss or incident or have merely adjusted to family life unwilling to address all the problems before them.

However, the sure fact is that you will never be able to resolve the worries and problems that come one on top of another when you take lightly the painful situations in your family. There is a limit to how many times you can avoid it, and you can only dodge your present reality for so long. The biggest factor in passing the spiritual problems in your family line along to the next generation is never having faced up to the problem. Of course, facing the problem does not mean we can solve the problem by our own effort but it is better than avoiding the problem or pretending that it does not exist.

Know that humankind's problems began in the family. Satan attacked Adam and Eve's family. He deceived them saying that if they ate the fruit of the knowledge of good and evil, they would become like God and the first people, Adam and Eve, became caught up in that deception. Afterwards, problems came into the family and rather than being resolved, they were passed down to the next generation and worsened as time progressed.

Find God's plan through all the things and meetings you face in your background and upbringing. Be able to hear God's voice. As much pain and heartache you receive from the adversities and problem you face, embrace God's plan deeper. To the point that it becomes your consuming passion. As you look at your parents, as you spend time with your siblings, and interact with your family members, you will be able to find their characteristics and flaws. Find God's plan within all that and hold to the covenant. Then our good God will absolutely answer and give realization. Parents who have unmarried children, pray for the marriage of your children. Young adults keep in mind the next section and pray for your marriage.

Marriage is important, then how do we go about it?

As you pray for marriage you must clearly look into your spouse' walk of faith. Date, travel together, and watch movies but do not lose hold of the time you spend sharing and talking about your faith. Examine each other's attitude towards life and your distinct characters. It is also a good thing to know if this person could not develop their clear talent because they did not have a conducive environment or whether this person is lazy and procrastination is instilled in their being and reflects in everything they do from their studies to their work. Also discuss each other's view of finances. Exchange your views about finances and talk about how you will manage your finances and offering.

They say that failure is the mother of success but our present reality clearly shows that not every experience of failure leads to success. In the same way, it is not the person who comes from difficult circumstances who succeeds but the one who finds his own answer within the failure-bound circumstances who will succeed. Once again think about the reason why it must be the Gospel and try to fathom how deep is the salvation you have received. The world is not that easy a place because the forces of sin, curses, and Satan are always squirming about. Take up the stance of fighting the spiritual battle and prepare for the great answers you will receive in the future.

Organize the things you need to do now and attempt them over and over again until they become your habit. Make the Word you received through weekly worship and everyday personal worship put down deep roots in your conscious and unconscious so that you will remain steadfast no matter what the situation. When two people like this come together as a family, they will be amazingly used by God.

Good-bye conflicts!

Conflicts arise anytime, anywhere regardless of age or gender. There are many times you feel like you will burst because of the spiteful friend who talks behind your back at school or the conflicts that arise because you simply cannot communicate with your parents. Whether it is the office superior who is always out to get you or the colleague who only thinks about himself; conflicts seem never-ending. Moreover, it is not only in the field. There are people who get on your nerves even at church. As time progresses, the people may change but conflicts from interpersonal relationships will always exist. How can you escape from this? Is there really a way out?

To begin with the conclusion, there is no way to get rid of conflicts, since people do not all think the way you think. However, you can overstep conflicts. Change your spiritual state. When you have spiritual strength, you gain the strength to overstep the various problems life throws at you. Then how can you enjoy this spiritual strength?

Lightly shake off the conflicts and get up again

First, you need the strength to enjoy the Gospel. As you live your life, you will face difficulties and things you simply cannot understand. Moreover, it is not that easy to see the answers within conflicts with people. Struggling to solve the problem will not solve the problem; it actually gets worse. At this time, lay everything down and focus only on the Word. If you enjoy the Gospel when conflicts come, you will be able to overcome the mountain load of conflicts in your field. Whenever you face a conflict, before asking, "What is wrong with that person?" or "What is wrong with me?," think about the strength God has given to you. Like the members of the Antioch Church, God will give the same strength to overcome tribulation to those who have the Gospel. The vexing conflicts will become the opportunities to receive blessings in the Gospel.

Conflicts, one step closer through the Gospel

Were there no conflicts or hardships in the Antioch Church

or the Early Church? It was probably worse than it is now. The reason why the Antioch Church and the Early Church left their mark in history amidst the unspeakable suffering and persecution they faced was because they stood on the line of the evangelist. The people, who saved the age throughout history, received the greatest answer regardless of their circumstances or problems. When you stand on the line of the evangelist amidst hardships, you will receive absolute answers. When you enjoy the Gospel regardless of the conflicts in your field, you rightfully stand on the line of the evangelists. Evangelism is what God fulfills when you enjoy the Gospel. When things do not work out the way you planned between your friends or when you are scarred by people, spend some time alone and quietly meditate on the Word. God will touch your heart and give you the strength to wisely resolve the issue.

Even today, the people you dislike are after you again. You have no idea what you did but it seems as if looking for some way to scar you is their calling in life. The words you want to rain down on them rise to the tip of your tongue but you use all your might to swallow them down again. Take a moment to breathe and hold to today's Word. As you follow God's plan and Word within the conflicts and hardships, God will grant you rightful, inevitable, and absolute answers.

Break the strongman

Recently a criminal who raped and murdered several women was arrested. He looked normal on the outside but his shameless demeanor and unremorseful smile shocked the nation. The diagnosis of "psychopath" does little to explain his atrocities or bring closure to the hearts of victims and their families. How should we accept the endless problems arising in the world?

The Bible gives the simple answer. All of mankind's problems began the moment they were deceived by Satan and separated from God. 1 Samuel 16:15-23 states than an evil spirit tormented King Saul's heart. Satan's deception crept into his heart, casting gloom and darkness over his thoughts and clouding his sense of judgement to the point of committing murder. The reason a thief sneaks around is because he knows that what he is doing is wrong. Even though he knows that what he is doing is not right, he keeps going down that path. This is because he is overtaken by the forces of darkness. The forces of darkness creep into your heart, prevent you from escaping the snares of suffering, and even ruin your health through disease and substance dependency. Even now, Satan attacks people so that they will not be able to believe in God. He especially hinders God's works and attacks so that the church cannot operate as a church should and the believer cannot live like a believer should. Then what must you do to break Satan's strategies?

Stop being fooled

In Acts chapter 12, Peter was imprisoned and the believers earnestly prayed to God for him. It would have been easy for them to be disappointed and discouraged from just looking at the situation, but they were not deceived. Satan wanted the Early Church to tremble and scatter in fear but rather, they came together as one. In the past, Peter denied Jesus in front of a small servant girl, but after realizing the Gospel, he was no longer afraid, to the point that he was able to sleep peacefully even though he was locked in prison!

Those who know who Jesus Christ is and believe in Him have surely received salvation; so stop being deceived. Those who

God will not let go.
He firmly holds the hand of the child
who stamps his feet and plops down saying,
"It's too hard," "I can't take another step!"

You do not have to throw a tantrum.
With a pleased smile, He watches over your steps.
You are doing just fine.

accept Jesus have the right to become children of God and the Jesus who has all authority in heaven and on earth, promised the filling of the Holy Spirit stating that we would be His witnesses. Some people say their incurable disease was healed after they believed in Jesus and some say they gained a peace they never felt before. Some people even say that life truly is worth living now that they believe in Jesus. It seems to be working for everyone else, even the person you considered the worst in all the world has changed. Then is your problem the only exception? Do not be deceived.

Boast about your background

God's promises are amazing. God said that He would send the offspring of woman to crush the head of the serpent.Genesis 3:15 All those who entered the ark, did not die, no matter who they were.Genesis 6:14 This is the promise given to us living in the culture of the world which the forces of darkness shake this way and that. There is no reason to become arrogant over the authority and privilege given to you as a child of God but there is no reason to cower in front of the world or be afraid of the forces of darkness either.

Just as God sent His angel to Peter while he was sleeping, God sends His ministering spirits[angels] to help your children.[Hebrews 1:14] God sent His angel ahead of Moses as he led the Exodus and He sent His angel ahead of Daniel as well. Remember this fact! If you do not enjoy the authority you have already been given, you will become lost in lethargy deceived by your own thoughts. This is the very foothold Satan is eyeing. As king Hezekiah prayed, God sent His angel and struck down the 185,000 soldiers of the Assyrian army. Remember the fact that angels take all the prayers of God's children up to God.[Revelations 8:3-5] This is your background! Strut around, fully use this and boast about it!

Not a theory, the real thing

There are people who do not acknowledge the existance of the forces of darkness. However, they are oblivious to the fact that they themselves are deceived. Perhaps it may seem "rational" to think that something does not exist because you cannot see it but the forces of darkness invisibly plow into the world to delude the world and break down families. People's hearts are becoming more desolate, the culture continues to grow more shocking, and the world is becoming more wicked everyday. The devil's activities will continue until the day Jesus returns, but the forces of darkness lose their strenth when we command them in

Jesus' name; each time we call on the name of Jesus, the forces of darkness flee.

Remember, your status has already gained the victory, so stop being deceived by Satan. Instead be the person of faith that makes Satan nervous. Gain the unlimited strength the Holy Spirit gives. Enjoy the firm spiritual background that will be your strong shield.

Give Him no rest

• Isaiah 62:6~7

On your walls, O Jerusalem, I have set up watchmen;
all the day and all the night they whall never be silent
You who put the Lord in remembrance, take no rest
and give him no rest until he establishes Jerusalem
and makes it a praise in the earth.

Give Him no rest

If you look in Isaiah chapter 62, it almost seems as if we could actually move God. How can we fathom the heart of God which so desires to teach us to pray?

God's child must understand the greatest priviledge the child of God can enjoy; we must understand prayer. Escape from the superficial mentality that thinks "I guess He'll answer if I pray" and be able to pray in your present reality. To enjoy prayer in your everyday life means to experience your own God, not your pastor's God or your mother's God. Praying "morning and night" means to pray 24 hours a day, then can we actually pray all day long?

God always remembers the prayers of His children. "You who put the Lord in remembrance."Isaiah 62:6 If you enjoy this blessing, you will fully triumph no matter where you go, who you meet, or what you face. Even if the forces of darkness try to hinder you, it will not be problem. If you know the mystery of prayer then everything is in God's hands and God will take responsibility whether it be the pastoral ministry of the pastor, the studies of the students, or the tournaments of the athletes.

There are people who remain in my heart even though a long time has passed since I met them in the evangelism field. They continue to challenge me in my walk of faith. There was one person who pledged to become a missionary when he was in college. He got a job at a bank and when he was promoted for his skill, he remembered the vow he had made in the past. He said that he could do missions once he became old and had nothing left to do here but he wanted to keep the promise he made to God while he was still young and could serve. I was so refreshed and challenged by his words. Another person ran an after-school academy. She never passed out any advertisement flyers for her academy; she just entrusted everything to God and prayed but her academy was the most popular academy in the entire city. However, there was always something that bothered her. "I want to proclaim the Gospel, but I don't know how to evangelize." Meeting people facing spiritual hardships because they do not know the Gospel burdened her heart with the passion for proclaiming the Gospel but she was so frustrated because she did not know how to evangelize. Seeing people like these helped me sense a little bit of God's heart.

How should we pray? Just pray from your heart. It is better to pray from your heart to God than trying to fill up the hours with prayer. This is because prayer is our faith. Do not forget the Words God gives you through your weekly worship. You may think that your prayer topics will get longer the more you listen to the Word but in actuatlity, they become more organized and concise. The more you know how much God loves you, how amazing the blessing you have received is, your inner self becomes more abundant and plentiful. When that happens you can enjoy the answers and blessings in the fields of your life. In this way, you can carry out your mission while enjoying the happiness of prayer. Go through, go through the gates; prepare the way for the people;

built up, build up the highway; clear it of stones; lift up a signal over the peoples.Isaiah 62:10

God has called you as the main figure for this age. Stand as a watchman of prayer. Enjoy the joy of prayer to the extent that you are acknowledged by God, people will nod their heads in agreement, and even the forces of darkness will hesitate before you. Open wide the treasure chest you have kept buried for so long. Do not keep the treasure of prayer locked up; take it out now and give God no rest from working with His powerful hands.

So now what must you do?   213

24, 1440, 86400

Reading a story or watching a movie with a long narrative, may leave you overwhelmed by the story for several days. As your emotions are swayed from empathizing with the main character, you can get lost in sadness and you lose your composure, or you can become overly excited for no particular reason. You may even get lost in your imagination wondering what would happen if the situation in the book or movie were real. If this is how easily we humans are influenced by a single book, a single movie, then trying to stand our ground without becoming swept up by the ever-changing world, public opinion, and culture seems quite difficult. If you take a closer look, most people live their lives without any answers. We are always searching for answers, "How should I live?" "Am I doing the right thing?" "Is the right time to move?" "Is he or she the 'one'?" but are frustrated because they are unclear. We know that "Jesus is the Christ" but sometimes that answer does not seem to have any realistic application in our lives. This is the reason I began to use the phrase "24 hour prayer." Some may ask, "Does that mean we should pray all day long?" This does not mean we should do nothing else but pray like some kind of guru. The key point of 24 hour prayer is that we can actually do something to overstep the level of our lives. The reason in using the phrase "24 hour prayer" is to emphasize the fact that answers already await God's children. God does not rest for even one moment; that is, He answers and works 24 hours a day. It is simply that we did not know it and have not seen it. The nature of doubting, laziness, running ahead, and meddling prevent us from knowing this. The thoughts that "Things will not work out since they haven't worked out so far," "There is no way answers will come to someone like me" blocks us from seeing the answers. Even though the answers are right in front of us, we cannot see them because of our attempts at saving face, our desire to be acknowledged by people, and the avarice of wanting to succeed. Therefore, we are helpless before the problems that come crashing in on us.

What fills your head

What is firmly lodged in your head and heart? The message

that is firmly embedded, inscribed like a seal in your head, is what moves your life. A person with "gambling" inscribed in his head will think of nothing but gambling no matter where he goes or what he does. Completely consumed by the thoughts of spreading out the cards or putting up the ante, he is driven by the assurance that, one day, he will hit the "big one."

The person who has "shoes" inscribed in his head, only sees shoes wherever he goes. Everyday, they while away the hours wondering what kind of shoes people are wearing and where they will find the next pair to add to their collection. They are glued to the store windows and search through countless online shops to find that one pair they like.

In the Bible, Genesis 6:8-9 states that Noah walked with God. The message that God was with him was embedded in Noah's heart. In Genesis 13:18, Abraham begins to build an altar before God. Abraham realized that he could not do anything without God's power. In Genesis 37:1-11, Joseph had an amazing dream. He dreamt that his brothers and parents bowed down to him; He knew "24 hour prayer". He believed that it was God who sent him ahead and not his brothers who sold him into slavery. In Psalm 23:1-6, we can see how David overcome the harsh circumstances and adversities. David believed, confessed and confirmed moment-by-moment, "the Lord is my shepherd." In Psalm 103:20-22, he was able to see the angels that carry out God's will and Word and he received God's guidance and rule.

Take a look at Daniel 6:16. King Darius said to Daniel, who was in the den of lions, "May your God, who you serve continually, deliver you!" In Daniel 6:20, the king returns to the den of lions to see what had happened to Daniel and asks "O Daniel, servant of the living God has our God, whom you serve continually, been able to deliver you from the lions?"

In King Darius' eyes, the God that the faithful Daniel believed, was not a god he believed for show but the true and living God. That is why he was sure that God would save Daniel. No wonder, he raced out there early in the morning to see what had happened!

What is inscribed in your head and heart? What kind of influence do I have over the people around me?

Prayer is not hard labor

God did not give us prayer to add one more burden to our already stifling life. Prayer is confirming the reason for your existence every single day. "24 hour prayer" is never forgetting the reason you live: every hour, every minute, and every second.

God called you and saved you as His child, so you can enjoy blessings no matter where you go. All your meetings will change into blessings. So now, connect all the people you think about and all your thoughts to prayer. There will be a time when you consciously "think" about something but more often thoughts just "come to mind." We may consciously think about "that person," but the face of the one we love just crosses our mind and fills our hearts. This is the central point of prayer. Always thinking about God because it is so wonderful that He is with you, being thankful that thoughts of Him cross your mind; this is it. This is hitting the bull's-eye in regards to your walk of faith.

Are you facing a problem while living your walk of faith? You have just seen a topic you can pray about. Have you ever prayed about the problem right before your eyes and received an answer? There is a difference between just worrying and having God rule over your thoughts. Hardships at church, interpersonal relationships, unspeakable family circumstances, financial hardships, there is no need to nitpick over the type or severity of the problem. As you focus and pray in detail, you will be amazed at the answers you gain. God will grant you answers, allow you to hear His Word, and show you the way to the extent that the word "amazing" will not do justice.

Are you complaining? Do you feel like there is nothing to be thankful for? Do you resent your husband, your wife? Are you disappointed by your parents? Does worrying about your children keep you up at night? Restore deep prayer. Gain tremendous strength and find the answer to your storm-tossed life. God did not heal the crippled man's legs and then tell him to get up. He said, "Get up and walk!" to the man who had never walked a day in his life. It is the same for you. He does not split the sea in half and tell us to cross over. The waves billow towards you ready to engulf you, but God tells us to cross this sea. It is at that moment, He sees our faith.

Go with the rhythm

People say, "Move your body to the rhythm" or "Go with the rhythm" to express when your body moves to the beat of the music and you find yourself nodding your head or tapping your feet in time with the music. I want to use rhythm as a final comparison to prayer. Find your own rhythm of prayer. Experience the rhythm of prayer in your body. There are various methods for doing this and it will differ from person to person.

My own method is to use deep abdominal breathing. With just a dozen breaths, sweat flows down my brow and back and my heart beats faster, improving circulation and clearing my head. I pray while doing these breathing exercises everyday. I reflect on the day's events and think about the people I will meet. I think about the things I must tell them or ask God for wisdom.

Some people may pray deeply while playing an instrument. Some people say they can concentrate in prayer when they jog through the park and others say they enjoy praying while driving to work in the morning. For some, it might be easy to pray while writing down your ideas and schedule notes while others find it peaceful to pray while trekking through the mountains. Some might find it cozy to pray crouching on the bed with the covers pulled over you, while some say the best time to pray is when you are sitting in the bathroom and can brush away all the petty worries. You can modify this day by day depending on your condition. There were even times when I was able to experience prayer more deeply because I was completely worn out. The more you pray, the clearer your soul becomes, the more organized your thoughts become, your heart gains stability, and even your body is refreshed.

God's kingdom comes

Now, if you have found the reason why you must live and

pray, then you can do fasting prayer or go to the prayer retreat center to pray. That is, if you want to put aside the comfort of eating and resting comfortably and focus on God. Do you want to know the secret to overcoming this progressively wicked world and the "you" that is so easily distracted? The answer is Acts 11:14.

If you receive the filling of the Holy Spirit, you can overcome all things. If God's kingdom comes within the boundaries of your life, your lifestyle, then you can overstep your level. You will be able to easily overstep the circumstances in your life just like the members of the Early Church, who fearlessly gathered even in the face of death to pray for the filling of the Holy Spirit. The work of the Holy Spirit fell upon all those gathered in Acts 2:1 like fire and like wind. How can people make the wind stop or start blowing? The works which no one could block arose. To receive the apostles' teachings, fellowship, and break bread with one another means that they were able to overstep their individual judgments of the people gathered in the church. The impossible conditions, surroundings, the people with various tempers and personalities were not stumbling blocks at all. This was possible because the promised Holy Spirit came.

Looking at them, people said, "They are filled with new wine." Some people act differently when they are drunk. There was a shy man in my town who changed into a chatterbox every time he drank. He would talk constantly, saying the same thing over and over again, curse, and pick fights. The man I knew seemed to have vanished without trace.

That the people filled with the Holy Spirit looked like they were drunk in the eyes of the unbelievers means that they had changed and seemed completely different than their former selves. Do think "but not me" and faint in surprise when the great answers come. What you need right now in your downright dreadful situation is the filling of the Holy Spirit. If you do not have the time of immersing yourself in God, you will chase after the people going ahead of you or be swayed by the seemingly flashy world and culture. However, the person who deeply communicates with God and focuses their every nerve to know God's plan, finds the standard of his life. He is not shaken by people's words or the ever-changing circumstances. He lives enjoying the kingdom of God. This is the true form and charisma of God's child.

Have you ever felt that cooking dinner for 3 minutes in the microwave seemed to take forever? However, 1 hour seems to fly by when you watch your favorite show on TV? The time you spend does not seem like a waste and rather, you feel it ended too quickly. I am sure you have felt times when the 1 minute you spend doing nothing seemed longer than the 60 minutes you spent completely absorbed in something.

How will you fill your today, your 24 hours, 1,440 minutes, 86,400 seconds? Answer this question, find the prayer method that best suits you, and pray; you life will be completely transformed.

Experience
God's love
through

First publication   November 25, 2013
Second publication   May 30, 2017

Author Ryu, Kwang Su
Publisher Joo, Suk Yun
Editor Bae, Jeong A; Yoo, Jae Un; Go, Ji Yeon
Design Bae, Eugene; Yoon, Ji Hyun; Kim, Do Hee
Marketing Lee, Hyun Shin; Jung, Won Kyu
Life Book Publications

Registration 109-91-23967

Address #202 41-34 Gonghangdaero Gangseo-gu Seoul, 07587 South Korea
Phone (02)3662-3881
Fax (02)3662-7149
ISBN 978-89-91848-55-9 *03200